VISIONARY LEADERSHIP
FOR CHURCH GROWTH

Dr. Carl Davis, Sr.

RELENTLESS
PUBLISHING

Visionary Leadership for Church Growth
Copyright © 2019 by Dr. Carl Davis, Sr.

Published by :
Relentless Publishing House, LLC
www.relentlesspublishing.com

RELENTLESS
PUBLISHING

ISBN: 978-1-948829-38-0

First Edition: February 2020

10 9 8 7 6 5 4 3 2 1

Dedication

I dedicate this study to my father, Samuel Carl Davis. My father's integrity, humility, love, compassion for the church, and for all people, left an impression on my life. I will be eternally grateful for the example he set for my family and me. To my wife Leslie, the woman of my dreams and my best friend. I dedicate this book and my life to her. She amazes me more and more every day. When God gave you to me he gave me the very best. Your unconditional love and enthusiastic spirit have made me into the man that I am today. I love you.

To my sons Nokomis, Carl Jr., Samuel, and Christopher, and my daughter Ashley, you all bring me an abundance of joy, and being your dad is my greatest reward. To two other people of Greater New Jerusalem Church, your love, loyalty, support, and enthusiasm are second to none. I am committed to you, and committed to helping you live your best life. Our greatest days are ahead. Finally, to my mentors Mr. and Mrs. David Rodriguez. You both encouraged me to continue to study the word of God, to reach the highest heights by being God's pupil; to learn His commands and statues, while enabling me to teach others how to be as Christ. I thank you both.

Abstract

Leadership in any organization is important. Leaders instruct others how to accomplish their assigned duties. Their leadership ensures the achievement of goals and objectives. Church leaders are essential because they teach their congregation how to grow spiritually. Leadership in the church can be assumed by the pastor, assistant pastor or any other person appointed or ordained to lead the congregation.

Visionary leadership guides others down a spiritual path which in turn results in the effective building of the church. This research seeks to unearth the importance of visionary leadership when planting churches. It examines the most significant ways that can be adopted by church leaders to ensure successful church planting, growth and expansion (Block, 2009). A purposive sample of 12 Christian ministers will be recruited for a 30 to 45 minute semi-structured interview.

TABLE OF CONTENTS

CHAPTER ONE

INTRODUCTION

Leadership in any organization is important because leaders teach others how to accomplish their assigned duties. Leaders ensure the goals and objectives set by the church are fulfilled. Church leaders are essential for the church to grow spiritually. Leadership in the church can be assumed by the pastor, assistant pastor or any other person appointed or ordained to lead the congregation.

Visionary leaders guide others in God's ways, which results in the effective building of the church. For a church to grow effectively and efficiently the pastor must teach others how to grow spiritually. A pastor with a vision clearly sees the needs of his congregation and explains how to meet those needs. A church will grow when it comes together to worship God and cheer each other towards attaining eternal life (Chant, 2012a, p. 67). Therefore, a church leader should create and sustain a vision the congregation understands. This chapter introduces what leaders need and explains the purpose of the vision in planting, growing and expanding churches in the contemporary Christian world.

Planning the expansion of a church needs proper leadership that ensures spiritual direction to achieve the church's mission, vision, goals and objectives. It is important for the pastor to build a vision that is inspiring and offers something new. As a leader or a pastor, it is crucial to map out the direction the church takes to grow numerically and expand geographically. Therefore, a leader has the vision to see a small church growing and expanding. By utilizing management and leadership skills the pastor can successfully guide a congregation to fulfill God's purposes.

Church growth and expansion is challenging. Many pastors and church leaders lack leadership skills and visionary strategies that produce church growth and meet the spiritual needs of the congregation. A church's vision sets its destination. As such the leader should establish steps that enable the church to reach its desired destination. It is important for the leader to emphasize the vision of the church and the actions necessary to attain that vision. Furthermore, a balance ought to be created when the direction of a church is being established.

The church leader should motivate and encourage the congregation to seek spiritual solutions for their problems (Langley & Kahnweiler, 2003). Members of the congregation need to be encouraged to find spiritual and biblical solutions to their problems. Through a visionary strategy, a leader can create an environment that motivates the congregation to worship as a team. An enabling environment creates positive attitudes that make attaining the vision a realistic goal to work toward. Furthermore, by creating an enabling environment the congregation learns how to motivate others to grow spiritually.

This research examines the most significant ways to ensure successful church planting, growth and expansion. For successful church growth to be realized the entire congregation must follow the church's mission, vision and goals. Therefore, a visionary leader needs to develop a formidable team. It is essential to provide an opportunity for each member of the church to participate. Their participation enables achievement of the goals, objectives, mission and vision of the church as a team.

Becoming an effective and visionary leader begins by following the example of successful leaders. Therefore, in visionary leadership the fundamental practice of following is very important. Following precedes and develops a leader's ability to achieve his or her desired results. Christ commanded all Christians to follow his example, and it is important for a church leader to imitate Christ as he strives to attain the church's mission and vision. Leaders are required to be an example. A leader must adopt practical and prophetic visionary leadership skills. Visionary leaders are able to engage equally with his peers in leadership and with the average church member. A church leader must build up all the people around him and ensure that they follow the policies that enable them to grow together.

For church leaders to be effective, they need mentors. Mentorship is a very important virtue in the church. It is of great significance for the church leaders to look for mentors and works towards achieving church leadership principles based on values extracted from the mentor. A mentor is someone who sets worthy objectives, establishes effective strategies, and implements the planned activities in a more effective manner.

Leaders matter in church planting and growth. To be a good leader, one should follow the example of Jesus Christ. By following the example of Jesus Christ, a church leader will learn humility, that is, how to treat people with the heart of a servant. The leader will also learn the virtue of perseverance, that is, how to endure adverse circumstances or suffering without losing joy. A church leader such as Pastor Paul Earl Sheppard can be a very important mentor to a church who wants his or her church to grow. Sheppard has been preaching since his teenage period and has been in the pastoral ministry since the year 1982. He has been serving as associate pastor of West Oak Lane Church. His humility, principles and leadership skills has enabled the West Oak Lane Church grow and prosper. Therefore, when one chooses him to be his or her mentor, he will be in the position to grow and become a very good leader.

A church leader also needs to understand the bible. The heart of a leader requires a love that will get involved in the messes and struggles which are being faced by the church followers. By reading and understanding the bible, leaders will be in the position to pick the most important topics which allow them to address those challenges. Understanding the bible is very important to a church leader in that he or she will get a clear understanding of the nature of the leaders. Furthermore, there will be a sense of self-awareness which is very important for any church leader. Therefore, a leader who understands the bible will follow the example of Christ as seen in the 1st Corinthians 11:1 where Apostle Paul says "Follow my example, as I follow the example of Christ." It is very important for the pastors and church leaders to understand what God requires them to do to ensure the needs of all the congregation have been adequately addressed.

Effective leaders also need to be likeable. All leaders fight to be at least liked and respected by the followers. However, leaders including the church leaders need to know that execution, getting the job and done at the right phase is very essential thus just trying to be popular. Church leaders ought to lead the congregation towards the right direction and adopting right leadership skills and knowledge. Visionary leaders who aspire to be liked by his or her followers should adopt leadership traits such as politeness, respectfulness and listening skills. Through such traits, an individual will boost the chances of leadership and success. It is of great significance for the leader to understand that effective and respected leaders do not have a big gap between what they say and what they do. Therefore, telling of the truth is very critical and mandatory than just telling people what they ought to hear as such results in a loss of trust in the leader among the congregation.

Therefore, proposals will be made that encourage church leaders to acquire the skills and strategies that enable them to plant, grow and expand the church in the contemporary Christian world. Furthermore, this research is crucial in that it provides solutions to solve problems which exist in the current church. Many churches face various problems due to poor leadership. Through this research church leaders will sharpen their skills to successfully lead a congregation.

History and Background of the Problem

The styles of leadership in traditional churches often vary from one leader to another. Some leaders copy styles based on the unquestioned rule of a king, queen or dictator. These styles hinder the spiritual and numerical growth of the church. In addition, the Bible gives an account of leaders who in one way or the other failed to lead their congregations in the right way. For example, Abraham endangered his wife when he lied and told her to lie about their relationship as husband and wife. Therefore, some leaders might copy his example and deceive their followers, which at the end may result in failed churches. Furthermore, the Bible also provides an account of Aaron deceiving his congregation when he made a golden calf and led the people to worship it rather than pointing to them to worship and praise God alone. Therefore, many people sinned because of poor leadership adopted by Aaron. These types of leader do not have visionary leadership skills that enable them lead the congregation in achieving spiritual and church growth. Moreover, historical records show that many churches in different areas of the world failed because of poor leadership from styles adopted by the pastors and other leaders in the church.

According to many scholars when new churches are led by leaders who lack visionary leadership skills the churches fail to grow spiritually. For example, in the Denver area, many of the failed church plants are attributed to ineffective leadership. The leaders were not in the position to lead others towards understanding the vision and the mission of the church to plant and grow new churches. Some pastors or church leaders also misappropriated funds meant for the church's growth and expansion (McCoy, 2005, P. 67).

In the United States of America, statistics shows the same pattern of failed leadership. The majority of people who seek leadership positions are motivated by fame and money instead of a passion to grown the church. Therefore, they lack visionary skills. Many scholars have written that despite the abundance of church plant trainings and assessments done in America many leaders still fail to ensure successful planting, growth and expansion of the church. They attribute such failures to church leaders who do not have visionary leadership skills, which is a prerequisite for planting and growing a church.

In England, for the past four decades, many churches and a network of churches which were planted and failed have taught the current churches styles of poor leadership. Some church pastors in England failed to adopt visionary leadership skills, which are crucial in ensuring successful church growth and expansion. Most church plants in England experience difficulties because of poor leadership and management skills adopted by pastors, church leaders and other stakeholders.

Financial resource management has become an issue in most churches across England. When financial resources are poorly managed in church institutions new churches fail to grow and attain its mission and vision.

Moreover, many churches in the United States of America planted during the 1980s had lead pastors and a core team who disagreed on theological issues making it difficult to walk together. That made it hard for new churches to grow, expand and realize its spiritual missions and visions. Therefore, people in church leadership positions have historically resulted in failed church plants and growth.

Historically, visionary leadership is depicted by the growth of New Creation Evangelical Lutheran Church in Lima. Initially, the church had a small congregation. The visionary leadership style adopted by church leaders produced a large congregation. Accordingly, New Creation Evangelical Lutheran Church currently has a core lay group that has seen the church grow and expand to reach different parts of the world. Importantly, they have lacked the failures experienced by other churches in property and financial management.

Because the group consist of visionary leaders, the future of the church is expected to be strong and has a spiritually foundation that will eventually win the hearts of many people across the world (McCoy, 2005). The growth experienced by adopting the visionary leadership style provides an opportunity to understand the importance of visionary leadership. Especially in the current church ministries where challenges are abundant and growth of the church is difficult. With visionary leadership the church will see an influx of new members who will then continuously engage in praise and worship and the eventual expansion of the church.

Research Questions

RQ1: What are Christian minister's perceptions of the potential for visionary leadership to address religious disaffiliation?

RQ2: How do Christian ministers implement visionary leadership constructs to address challenges?

Statement of Purpose

The purpose of the proposed qualitative case study is to explore the potential for visionary leadership growing religious disaffiliation. Christian ministries are faced with enormous challenges that make it difficult to accomplish their missions, visions, goals and objectives and grow their congregations (Hesselgrave, 1980). Through visionary leadership, the churches can address the challenges and then realize growth and expansion. Furthermore, visionary leadership enables the pastors and church leaders to guide members for successful planting and growth of new churches.

Nature and Scope of the Study

The proposed study will employ a qualitative case study research design to collect and analyze data from 12 Christian ministers regarding their perceptions of the potential for visionary leadership to address challenges. This study will be limited to visionary leadership and church growth. An analysis of Christian Churches in America will be undertaken. It will mainly study those churches that have succeeded after being planted verses those that have failed to grow. This analysis will bring to light the challenges faced by newly planted churches and already established churches and provide recommendations on how to overcome those challenges (Gonzalez, 1996, P.91). Through the examination of failed churches because of poor leadership and comparison with churches that have grown because of visionary leadership the study will offer solutions for churches that have been planted but failed to grow and expand.

Significance of the Study

This study explains the significance of visionary leadership when planting churches.

For a church to grow after being planted good leadership is required. A pastor or a church leader ought to have a vision and a clear understanding of the church's mission. As a leader, it is of great significance to possess visionary capabilities in order to bring change to the society and to those who are being led. Through visionary church leadership the way of doing things in the church will be improved and thus the performance of the church, company or any other group would be significantly improved. The blossoming of the church depends on the leaders who started planting it. A church may be facing several challenges and if the leaders are not prayerful, it might result in church failure. Leaders of the church should set the purpose and direction for the church to avoid things that discourage members from attending. (Gonzalez, 1996, P.66). Church leaders ought to understand that the church does not exist for itself. Church growth is very crucial because it acts as a vehicle that manages, nourishes and leads people to achieve spiritual growth. Leaders can enable a church to grow through organizing discipleship and evangelical missions. Thus, this study is important because it provides knowledge of how pastors and church leaders can motivate other members to achieve the established mission and vision of the church. This study is also important because it will unearth the capabilities and skills required in a church leader to lead a congregation and provide solutions to problems that might hinder the church from growing and expanding.

This study will also enable the congregation to understand that they are very important during church planting and growth. Thus, they can appropriately help church leaders in implementing objectives of the church. More importantly, congregations will understand that challenges are part and parcel of Christian lives but challenges should not hinder them from practicing their Christianity and planting churches in new areas.

CHAPTER TWO

LITERATURE REVIEW

This chapter reviews resources written by other scholars regarding visionary leadership for church growth and unearths a gap that exists about the subject. Recommendations on how to address the gap are offered. It also explores the problems faced by church plants churches and how those problems can be addressed. Visionary leaders in any institutions are inspired and driven by what an institution would like to achieve. Visionary leaders are people who see the big picture and do everything possible to achieve the established goals and objectives of the institution.

Visionary leaders are tactical. They lead the congregation towards the right direction. They characteristically bring a cohesiveness that inspires the congregation to achieve the set goals and objectives. In fact, church leaders who are visionary are characterized by their charismatic and determined motives that ensure the congregations are spiritually nourished. They are confident coaches who have the ability to guide others to achieve set goals and objectives.

Visionary leadership is the most common trait displayed by those who successfully lead congregations towards spiritual achievement. Vision is essential for success in life, church and also in ministry. It is crucial for church leaders to follow Christ's example (Langley & Kahnweiler, 2003).

For church leaders need to be skilled in the practical and the prophetic to be effective in guiding congregations (Baumgartner, 1990). Therefore, they must pragmatically work within the realm of reality by maximizing the available personnel and resources. Thus, they must treat people equally and be able to build up the people and platforms around them. Church leaders who have visionary leadership skills welcome their students achieving greater things knowing they will all attain the Kingdom of God. Practically, visionary leaders ought to study scripture to discover the attributes of leadership.

Developing new ministry initiatives that could result in growth of the church is the key skill all church leaders should possess. New initiatives are crucial to the church for obtaining growth and expansion. Understanding personal issues among the congregation can enable one to meet the spiritual needs. As a leader of a church, one has to understand significant challenges facing the church and provide adequate strategies for addressing those challenges. According to different scholars God himself offers the church with three types of leaders that enable the church to meet spiritual needs. Thus, God empowers all church leaders to undertake their respective roles and provide good leadership to the church members.

Research shows where there is no vision people perish. It is important to eliminate this problem by developing vision. Arguably, vision does not originate from the masses but it is initiated by the leader. A leader who has a vision for the church spends much of his or her time in Bible study, prayers and listening to the Holy Spirit. He or she examines the context of what the church is required to accomplish. For effective growth of churches, a leader must be in the position to develop and accomplish an action plan. A visionary leader should look to Moses example when he led the people of Israel out of Egypt. Because he was a visionary leader Moses handled problems in a more effective manner.

Therefore, it is important for the leader to understand personality issues of those who are faced by various challenges (Gonzalez, 1996, P.55). Growing churches involves developing a strategic plan which can easily be understood by members of the church. Furthermore, the leader must inspire followers with spiritual encouragements to be involved in the church's vision.

For planted churches to grow, expand and provide the right spiritual messages, the leaders need right leadership principles. Leadership should establish principles of accountability. Being accountable enables leaders to undertake the duties and responsibilities of the church in a more effective manner. Furthermore, the church leaders must understand the needs of church members. It is of great significance to understand God's purpose for the neighborhood the church influences. That can be gained by brainstorming with church members on the challenges and opportunities available. Pastors and spiritual leaders should also understand that establishing churches is God's purpose. Therefore, appropriate leadership is significant in church growth and expansion.

As Christians approached the 21st century, it was important to understand how to build churches that will eventually offer spiritual nourishment to all the church members regardless of their social backgrounds. DeKoven (1997, P.312) argues that it behooves pastors and church leaders as ministers of Christ to follow Jesus example in building and growing a church.

Several things are necessary to plant a church successfully (DeKoven, 1997, P.112). Leaders need to understand what scripture wants them to do and what God requires in the newly planted church. Throughout the book, DeKoven addresses questions which are related to patterns of today's divine blessings. Furthermore, the author argues that it is crucial for church leaders to understand the salient characteristics of blessed churches and work towards building those churches (DeKoven, 1997, P. 95). The book further provides an opportunity to know the driving force towards God's kingdom. Successful churches ought to learn from biblical teachings and should adhere to the fundamental patterns created by God in the Old Testament of the Bible.

According to Chant (2012b), successful Christianity creates an opportunity for the growth and expansion of the church. Christians and church leaders should only do what God requires them to do with regards to church growth and expansion. Doing anything that is not based on Christian values is ungodly. In particularly, the issues that impact church members and the basic principles should be adhered to for effective planting, growth, and maintenance of the church. The book is crucial as it offers principles of church planting and survival in a competitive world where sin has manifested itself greatly (Chant, 2012b, p. 99). Thus, when engaging in church planting, it is of great significance to teach church members how to avoid and overcome sin and live righteous lives. The presence of God is significant in fulfilling the great commission and prospering church growth and expansion.

Leadership enables church members to keep the church together and eventually they will realize the growth and expansion of the church. Church growth is measured by successful evangelism and the impact of a church in a particular society. Visionary leaders and pastors will focus on confident outreach for the expectation of continuous growth of church members.

"Word" is defined as an aspect that reveals God because it is the divine message from God. It is considered pure truth revealing the nature of God. The Bible reveals the will of God. The Word of God is thoroughly conveyed by the Bible writers to humanity who do not know anything about God (Fowler, 2008).

Gospel refers to the written accounts of the teachings and career of Jesus Christ. Furthermore, in Christianity "the Gospel" can be viewed in the book of Mathew, the book of Mark, the book of Luke and the book of John which record the truth about Jesus Christ, his teachings, his career, and his miracles. They are referred to as "gospel books" because they reveal the message about the life of Jesus Christ. The Gospel is the good news that teaches people how to live holy lives and believe in the message of Jesus. The Gospel is significant because it denotes the oral traditions, which are the sayings and stories passed to future generations as self-contained units which are separate and are not in order but they still talk about the supernatural existence of God (Williams, 1994). Furthermore, it is the gospel that teaches believers about miracles which were performed by Jesus Christ. Ideally, the Good News reveals Jesus Christ, the essence as well as the blessings brought about in his death and resurrection, and also instructs how everyone can be a partaker of these blessings. The core of the Gospel is centered on Jesus Christ being God who lived a spotless life here on earth, crucified as a result of false accusations, died and rose on the third day, in accordance to God's plan and His foreknowledge.

Church members will have a continuous life and blessing. More, importantly there will be a constant inspection to understand an individual's Christian status and know how to improve such Christianity which eventually provides the growth and expansion of the church (Chant, 2012b, p. 113). As the church grows its members will realize the importance of being together and building a living church. When church members encourage each other towards Christianity, they will be in the position to grow together as church members and build a community of believers.

In the book Understanding Church Growth an examination of how visionary leaders can engage in building an effective church is examined. The author uses empirical research and sociological principles to explain how evangelism strategy can be undertaken. According to the book, it is crucial for church leaders to engage in a continuous examination of various strategies which will ensure efficient church planting and eventual growth (Donald, 1970, P.45)

Since the outpouring of Holy Spirit at Pentecost church growth has been viewed as taking place in various forms. Ideally, it has been the central focus of Christian missions. For instance, the majority of the churches that grow have been linked to proper church leadership. Furthermore, revivals are strategies used by different leaders to ensure effective growth and expansion of the church. For churches to realize growth in various regions spiritual and biblical messages should be utilized. For instance, church leaders should teach members the importance of worshiping together especially when they are planting a church (Patzia, 2001, P.91). The work of the Holy Spirit has been seen as crucial in church planting and growth since time immemorial. Historically, believers have been planting, nurturing and ensuring that a church significantly grows through continuous prayer. It is an important thing for church leaders to direct the community of believers towards understanding the existence of Christ by engaging in deeper spirituality. Furthermore, a deeper understanding of the relationship between spirituality and church growth is the responsibility of church leaders.

The church as an organization becomes complex because of bureaucracy. Management sets rules to be followed when executing particular activities. The practice makes a team unable to achieve its objectives and goals because not all the workers are ready to follow and abide by such rigid business rules and regulations. Using structure and strategy adopted by businesses also makes it complicated. It is reported that many organizations have a complex structure that requires a high number of employees to execute the activities of a company. The article argues that the complexity of an organization is also witnessed when the company develops complex business strategies. Accordingly, it is of great importance for the organization to have proper leadership to execute and accomplished such business plans. Additionally, the methods used, and the products manufactured by a team also makes it complex. The planning, organizing and controlling processes also makes an organization complex.

Lightner (1995) explains that contemporary theology is very significant because it teaches the eternal truth about God. Therefore, a Christian will bear upon the contemporary considerations regarding the modern intellectual conditions. Lightner (1995) engages in the examination of ontology about God. Furthermore, he argues that forgiveness and truth in the modern world are very significant and provides an opportunity to the Christian to understand more about the existence of God (Smith, 2002). According to the author, theology tries to explain what God has revealed to the church and the Christian community. Evangelical theology reveals an evangelical perspective that emphasizes being born again and providing a personal relationship between the Christian and Jesus Christ (Elwell, 2001). Through evangelical theology, the evangelists engages in teaching and describing the evangelical approach to the Christian faith. Accordingly, the Bible is the sole authority for practice and faith in the life of Christians.

The author believes that evangelical theology places a strong emphasis on accountability and conversion in faith on a personal level. Every individual makes his or her decision. The new birth is significant because it proves the power of the gospel for salvation through missionary work. Through missionary work evangelists promote the gospel, and in most cases, they have been responsible for going around the globe to share the good news about Jesus Christ. Furthermore, through evangelical theology Christians influence laws and culture of the communities they visit. Therefore, the evangelist sets high morals and ethical standards and lead lives that are separated from sin. More importantly, evangelical theology focuses on the gospel of good news for the world in Jesus Christ (Barna, 2000). According to Lightner (1995), the Bible is the authoritative word of God and the foundational message of grace that imparts an understanding of the existence of God. Being a trans-denominational movement, evangelical theology maintains the essence of the Gospel consisting of doctrines of salvation through faith and the all sufficient grace in Jesus Christ.

The God Who Risks: A theology of providence explains that love is the most significant quality that human beings should attribute to God. According to the book love ought to be taken as more than just care and commitment. It is through the aspect of love that human beings are in the position to live together and provide care to one another (Sanders, 1998). A congregation shows moral support to those in need through love and commitment. Love in contemporary theology involves being responsive as well as being sensitive to the lives of other people (Sanders, 1998). The author argues that love determines an individual's relationship with others in the same society.

To have real choices, freedom is crucial. An individual's decisions regarding Christian faith cannot be foreknown. The future is not determinable, but in most cases, it is shaped by individual choices (Smith & Emerson, 1998). Therefore, unlike the past, the future is not known but shaped by the choices a person makes.

According to Sanders (1998), theologians should understand that the future is not fixed. Only God knows the future and therefore it cannot be infallibly anticipated. Therefore, future decisions cannot be foreknown. The author urges theologians to guide people to better choices and thereby shape a better future. First of all, theologians must be open to take full account of the biblical language about the foreknowledge of God, human love that influences the future, decisions made about the future, and God's existence in the human heart (Bloesch, 2008). Classical theists should take a full and robust biblical approach when they are taking about God and Gods defining moments. People should continuously read the scripture with the insights that are provided through historical interpretation of the biblical messages and writings (Sanders, 1998). They should constantly verify if voices are of God and provide a qualitative interpretation to those who lack an understanding of God's message to the church and society.

As a theologian, one must avoid the tendency towards individualism regarding biblical interpretation. Voices of the past should be considered when making plans to spread the gospel in foreign lands. As an evangelical theologian, the traditions about God's existence should be maintained and spread to other areas of the world (Church Growth International, 2009).

God is a risk taker (Sanders, 1998). For him, risk-taking is essential in contemporary theology. Taking risk put God in the position to relate on a personal level with humanity and other creations. God comprehensively controls all things because he created all things (Sanders, 1998). The "risk" view of providence starts with the assumption that if God is in some respects limited by his creatures, he takes risks in bringing about the particulars of the world (Sanders, 1998). However, God has created some particular boundaries through which the creatures can operate. Therefore, God's sovereignty is important to a theologian for achieving the defined responsibility of mutual relations and love for one another. Sanders (1998) book seeks to examine whether risks and relationship are intertwined. He believes humanity relates to God because the scripture provides a way for humanity to have a good relationship with God and that love should exist in such situations (Ware, 2000).

Pinnock's (2001) book articulates the defense of openness theology time immemorial to the present time. Pinnock offers a deep debate about the openness of God and the evangelical movement. Accordingly, he offers reactions and replies through the thinker's mind on how a good relationship with God can ensure peaceful coexistence among all people (Strohbehn, 2016). Classical theology assumes that changes only happen through God's operation. The gospel of God should be spread through contemporary theology and by the Christian (Pinnock, 2001). The contemporary theologian understands the changing views regarding the openness of God. Therefore, the leaders of the church keep the community abreast of the current evangelical changes regarding God's nature and attributes (Elwell, 2001).

God's Lesser Glory: The Dimension of God of Open Theism by Bruce Ware is an important book as it touches on how Christians throughout history have been strengthened by the knowledge that God understands everything about the future. Open theism is crucial because it adjusts the confidence in the future and God's existence. Therefore, people are motivated to leave everything in the hands of God. The result is facing the future with greater confidence in God. Moreover, open theism adjusts the whole picture of God's involvement in human lives and also adjust the picture of God's sovereignty. Ware summarizes and makes criticisms of dangerous doctrines from a biblical perspective. He, therefore, provides an excellent treatment of both the openness and the classical views about God's existence and his knowledge about the future. The implications of theism are made by Ware to compare open theism and classical theism (Ware, 2000). Through research Ware demonstrates different ways that undermine trust in God and therefore, undermine the Christians relationship and understanding God's supremacy.

Open theism acknowledges that God's understanding about the future has not been disclosed to humanity. Therefore, people are often surprised by events in society. Accordingly, freedom is possible only when we are free to choose. However, some open theists argue that if God knows human feelings, thoughts, and actions in advance, then there is no relationship with him (Ware, 2000). Such arguments are bad because they diminish the glory of God as the scripture states that God can know the future and what will befall humanity. Biblical teachings states that God is in control of everything including the future.

In the early days and during the foundation of the church Christian theology and belief was shaped by significant responsibilities geared towards the life of the church. Such important functions and responsibilities of the church included the catechetical, homiletical, polemical and apologetically based functions (Beek, Borght, & Vermeulen, 2010). These functions still exist in the contemporary church. The process of catechesis is known as discipleship in the current church. According to theological messages and scriptures the word of God is spread through current church ministries. Christian theology defends and expounds the biblical faith against threats which are considered heretical (Olson, 2003).

Contemporary theology, in most cases, has focused on areas such as gender equality in the community and the church. Some theologians argue that contemporary theology encourages feminists to indulge in religious leadership by ignoring the stereotype that women cannot take part in leadership positions. Over the years much attention has been placed on men engaging in leadership positions thus discriminating against women in society.

According to research such discrimination has extended to religious institutions. Furthermore, in contemporary theology philosophical trends have also been a point of interest. Issues relating to human rights, bioethics, faith in public and the environment have significantly been emphasized by contemporary theologians (Olson, 2003). Everything that is undertaken by theologians is significant because they focus on understanding the scripture and how God's word improves relationships. Accordingly, the word of God is living and active. Furthermore, it does not change with time, and therefore, contemporary theologians are called upon to show love towards each other. They are expected to encourage people to believe in the only creator of Heaven and Earth. The word of God spread by theologians is very important because it enables people to grow spiritually and live worthy lives.

Contemporary theology directly concerns the individual believer and provides a basis for assurance of salvation. Fundamental issues relating to the deity of Christ, the work of redemption, and the experience of divine grace are undertaken through contemporary theology. Theology that provides standards of absolute righteousness is very crucial for Christian relationships and engaging in other good things. The Bible is a crucial tool that teaches how God relates to humanity and how he rules his creation. Therefore, by spreading the word of God people will understand the existence of God. God's authority over creation demonstrates that God is the only Supreme Being and people should believe in Him. When an individual understands and believes in God, he receives an assurance of salvation.

Reframing can also be adopted by a church leader to grow and expand the church. Reframing deliberately looks at the larger perspective enabling an individual to avoid an oversimplified way of leadership. The frames include human resource, structural, political and symbolic frames. These are important because each of them examines the processes, skills and purpose of leadership which makes leadership successful. The process of reframing includes focusing on the work to be undertaken. A leader engages in reframing by focusing on the plan and organization of the activities which are intended to be executed. Furthermore, the reframing process also involves rethinking the relationship of environment and business strategy. This ensures that the leader motivates other workers towards achieving the goals and objectives of the company. Furthermore, the process of reframing involves the evaluation and adoption of new strategies. The process of reframing is significant to leadership because it provides an overview of what is expected of a leader and the processes of ensuring the church achieves the set goals and objectives. Leaders acquire their personal frame and preferences through believing and communicating with people who are within and outside the organization. Furthermore, when leaders become visible and accessible, they acquire their leadership frame preferences. Also, the leaders also acquire their personal frame preferences by empowering those who work with him or her. I have received my personal frame preferences after motivating my congregation to work together and ensuring that we achieve the set business goals and objectives as a team.

Reframing is important because it provides a platform to the leader to execute the assigned duties within the organization effectively. It looks at the organizational structure on a wider perspective and ensures the decision-making process is efficient. An example is when I chaired a team in a Houston Hotel tasked to solve a specific problem. We ran out of food, but we had not exhausted the customer orders. It was significant to assemble all the chefs to deliberate how to meet the client's demands within the deadline. Successful leaders always motivate others towards achieving set goals and objectives (Epes, 1948). It is known that when employees are motivated, they tend to work hard and always aim at achieving the best. Therefore, a leader should have a vision and share it with his team.

Christian education is also crucial. It is important because it instructs believers about Christianity. How they can conduct religious practices, and how to follow Christian doctrines to realize church growth and expansion. Pastors can communicate church planting intentions through missionary work and continuous prayer. Furthermore, Church growth will be realized when Christian leaders engage church members in scripture reading, devotions and sharing their faith (Lyall, 1994). Education about biblical scriptures and messages in church planting provide an opportunity to understand the challenges facing new churches and eventually offer solutions to those problems. That is an important way of enriching the church and ensuring that all the members are equally provided with greater opportunities to enjoy what the church offers them (Getz, Wall, Swindoll, & Zuck, 2000, P.32). The members will grow spiritually. Church leadership is also crucial to growing the church because they teach the members to see a greater harvest when people spread the word of God. Thus, leaders ought to understand that people can grow spiritually and through continuous prayer and working together church growth will be realized. Church leaders should teach members how to conduct prayer meetings so they can achieve common goals and objectives. Through teaching, leaders direct church members to walk toward a common course of Christian enrichment.

Visionary leaders are the builders of a new dawn. They are important in every situation because they offer solutions to challenges that call for effective leadership. In Christianity and church growth, leaders work with the power of intentionality and alignment with a higher purpose to ensure members of the church become spiritually mature. Their eyes are set on the horizon of spiritual growth and fulfillment. Because they are prayerful, they view the big picture of the overall church, challenges facing the church and how well they can handle those challenges through spiritual means. A pastor's vison offers solutions to spiritual problems.

Theology refers to the study of God's nature and religious beliefs as they are systematically established. Theology assumes that God exists in some form including the physical form, the supernatural form, the mental form and the social realities form. Theologians try to explain the nature of God by following such characteristics and experiences. On the other hand, the theology of the word refers to teachings of Holy Scriptures and the interpretation of components that best describes the nature of God. According to Mulholland, Anderson, and Anderson (2012), theologians try to explain the supernatural God by describing His characteristics including the physical form, the social realities that describe God and how God relates with humanity.

The Word is said to be without error because God cannot lie. The Word's domain is founded on the death and the resurrection of Jesus Christ who rules all things. If one rejects this fundamental truth he or she rejects God Himself. The core purpose of the Word is not to reveal the secrets of heaven but God's message which illustrates his creative authority and his redeeming love through his son Jesus Christ. God's wholesome relationship with his creation is established in his Word. Furthermore, the theology of the Word approach focuses pre-eminently on Jesus Christ as the Living Word. Jesus Christ who is the Living Word is holy and upright.

Secondly, the Word is the writings found in the Holy Scripture commonly referred to as the Bible, which comprises the Old and New Testaments. According to Bass & Briehl (2018), the Word proclaims Jesus Christ as the head of the church, which reveals his father through the Holy Spirit of God. In addition, the Word responds to all needs of humankind and the entire creation. Moreover, the Word is authoritative and redemptive.

The Word is significant to believers because it enables them to understand the nature of God and Jesus Christ who is the savior. Through evangelical approaches, people understand how God sent his only son to save humanity from sin. Historic Christian theology was the basis for dialogue established from a non-Christian belief system. It shows shared values can focus on two or more faiths, which can include the "Abrahamic faiths" comprised of Judaism, Islam and Christianity. It can also focus on the Eastern religions, which include Buddhism, Hinduism, and Christian movements. Therefore, the intellectual challenges such as social issues, scientific issues and religious practices and issues are examined, and viable solutions are provided through theological practices. Religious research shows that contemporary theologians share a common Christian heritage. Therefore, Christian institutions teach views regarding faith and belief in the contemporary society.

A visionary leader does more than speak. He or she also acts. Visionary leaders enable church members to attain spiritual transformation. When planting a church, visionary leaders normally plan what a church intends to bring to the environment where it has been established. Another important factor that leads to church or community growth and development spiritually is the focus on biblical teaching. The most relevant way of moving people in the church or the community forward is through engaging in biblical teaching (Barnard, 1993, P.145). Visionary leaders engage in spiritual and biblical teachings. It is always important for the church or spiritual community leaders to ensure regular biblical teaching in the church for it to realize growth, expansion and eventually provide spiritual needs to the members (In Lienhard, 2011). As a leader, it is significant to engage the church or the Christian community in Bibles study and they should be encouraged to study on their own.

For spiritual church growth, it is also important to clarify the role of the church and the Christian communities. People should be encouraged to mature in their belief and embrace personal development practices as part of their spiritual journey. Members should understand that a community of believers need to encourage each other towards spiritual growth and development (Langford, 1999, P.78). A spiritual leader or a pastor ought to encourage the congregation to reflect on scriptures and biblical teachings.

A visionary leader that aspires to grow and reach spiritual maturity focuses in missions. Growing churches involves establishing missions that spread the word of God. As the word traverses through different regions, spiritual development is encouraged that provides an opportunity for the members to attain spiritual growth and stability. Churches that do not focus on mission establishment will stagnate. Therefore, it is essential for pastors and spiritual leaders to realize the importance of Christian missions and thus establish them in their churches or the communities they lead (Fletcher, 2006, P.47). Leaders should also create church visions and missions which encourage members to become involved in nurturing of the church.

Qualities

An important quality among church leaders in charge of growing churches is emotional reasoning. Emotional reasoning refers to the ability for a person to use emotional information to make decisions (Bassey, 2018). Emotional information is created by individuals and the people around them. When a person is better able to gauge the feelings of others, they are able to make better decisions. Previous research has shown that the ability to make well informed decisions that include addressing the emotional states of others is important. Engaging others in shared tasks and teaching others are traits that a leader with emotional reasoning shares, and that completing these shared tasks and teaching others can help impart valuable knowledge and skills to others.

Effective church leaders are defined by the ability to not only manage the duties of others, but to motivate others and innovate new solutions to problems that arise. Watt and Voas (2015) indicated that it was also important for church leaders to be able to empathize with those around them. However, the researchers warned that placing to much of am emphasis on one attribute may come at the cost of another. In many cases, good people managers were not necessarily very empathetic, which was a particularly important trait for ministers. The researchers indicated that a minister's personality type often determined which particular traits they were strongest in. However, it was also noted that while a minister might not be strong in one trait, that trait could be developed through training.

Examination of the clergy in the Church of England indicated some personality traits were commonly associated with leaders who saw growth in their churches. Certain psychological profile types were most associated with church growth (Francis, 2016). Leaders with these traits were typically extraverted, intuitive, and perceptive. However, the researchers found that the opposite traits were most often found in church leaders. The profession seemed to attract individuals with the opposite personality types required to encourage church growth, though this was a study limited to one particular type of church. The study results still indicated that by finding leaders with certain personality traits, or at least encouraging those traits within leaders, that church growth might be encouraged (Francis, 2016).

A study within the Korean Catholic church also found several traits of leaders were associated with increasing member commitment to the church. Joo, Byun, Jang, and Lee (2018) surveyed church members across 28 Catholic churches. When traits associated with servant leadership were found, church members were more likely, members were more likely to be more committed to their church leaders and the organization. Servant leadership was characterized as by personality traits including awareness, empathy, persuasion, foresight, and commitment to the people, among other qualities (Joo et al., 2018). The research showed how certain behaviors and personality traits might encourage greater commitment to the church.

A quality that leaders may want to avoid adopting is the belief that they can encourage growth on their own. In some cases, church leaders begin to believe they, as solo actors, can encourage the growth of their churches (Fee, 2018). These leaders come to believe that they have to handle the growth of their churches independently, rather than relying on others to support their efforts. This approach to leadership often leads to burnout among leaders, which in turn creates less effective leaders.

Church Growth

Lam (2016) noted that there were a few characteristics that growing churches had in common. A stable pastor committed to the longer-term growth of the church is one of the qualities that growing churches possess. Pastoral leadership as noted as a decisive factor in determining whether a church would grow or become stagnant. Many of these pastors committed to a church for a period of between 10 to 15 years. At the same time, these pastors also influenced others, building relationships and eventually garnering support and finding allies to support their efforts to grow a church. In growing churches, leadership teams were developed that helped encourage church growth. These leaders were often capable of reaching out to individuals and motivating them to become church goers. Effective leaders put together plans to reach out to people and entice them back into the church. One way this as accomplished was through the creation of arm relationships with individuals. These warm relationships and the groups built around them helped to motivate individuals to return to church (Lam, 2016). Effective leaders also developed a system for developing future leaders within their churches.

The importance of long term commitment from leaders is especially important in light of how church growth traditionally occurs. Mathematic models suggested that church growth typically occurred rapidly during a period of revival and that church growth then slowed or regressed (Hayward, 2018). Typically, religious revival periods were marked by times of great enthusiasm. During this period, congregation members were the most enthusiastic and engaged. It was during this period that church members were most effective at recruiting new members, which was linked with church growth. As enthusiasm died down, church members became less effective at recruiting new members. Church growth was therefore characterized by enthusiasm, growth, decline in enthusiasm, and decline (Hayard, 2018). This model of church life cycles suggested that leaders needed to plan around such a cycle and implement long term plans for growth if they hoped to avoid stagnation.

Church growth and decline as also defined. Church growth was estimated to mean an increase of 5% in the congregation while church decline as estimated as 5% decline in congregation numbers (Cincala, McBride, & Drumm, 2017). Small churches were defined as those with under 100 members while midsized churches were defined as those with between 101 and 249 members. Large churches were considered those with over 250 individuals in attendance. The smallest churches were those most likely to experience decline, with 40% of small churches experiencing decline and 23% experiencing growth. Among midsized churches, 26% were in decline while 25% were in a state of growth, indicating that the majority of midsized churches ere plateauing. On the other hand, only 15% of large churches were in decline while 26% were in a state of growth (Cincala et al., 2017). Research pointed to large churches being the most likely to experience growth.

Church growth often comes up against what is called the 200 barrier. The 200 barrier refers to a common number in attendance at which a church starts to plateau and sometimes stagnate and decline (Douglas, 2019). Researchers have indicated that church growth shouldn't be encouraged for the sake of numbers alone. When churches reach more than 150 members, they typically start to slow in their growth. It is at this point that pastors and church leaders should begin considering what sort of barriers exist within their churches and how to address them for the sake of encouraging further growth. Leadership must be equipped with the skills necessary for addressing these barriers if they hope to break through the 200 barrier (Douglas, 2019).

Surveys seemed to show that there was a lack of leadership within those churches in decline. Abney (2018)indicated that many churches lacked leadership development across multiple capacities. Clergy themselves often went unmentored in almost all cases, indicating that many clergy took on their roles without first witnessing how to be leaders themselves. Researchers suggested that seminaries and academic institutions offering theological and divinity programs should offer ministers in training a chance to grow as leaders. As such, leadership development was important. More resources needed to be provided to leadership development programs at all levels, from universities to seminaries and church conference, to help better prepare ministers to be leaders once they began performing their duties (Abney, 2018).

Leadership development was noted more than once as important to the growth of church. A study of North Carolina churches suggested that leadership development and empowerment were both critical to encouraging church growth (Jordan, 2019). Leaders needed to pass on their knowledge and skills to others, which could lead to the development of leadership teams that might help to grow the church. Church leaders should identify leadership qualities in others, including important attitudes and personality traits. Researchers indicated that when senior pastors were active in leadership development, many saw growth within their churches. Leadership development plans were important to this kind of growth, with leaders creating plans for systematic leadership development (Jordan, 2019).

Part of encouraging further growth must include setting the strategic direction for a church. The ability for leaders to set a strategic direction was found to be influential in the growth of the church in Kenya (Mutia, K'Aol, & Katuse, 2016). It was considered important for leaders to be clear about the direction their organizations would take and how the organization's goals would be reached. Strategic direction begins with leaders, who establish the direction and methods of the church, which then filter down through the rest of the organization. Within church growth in Kenya, there was a strong connection between setting strategic direction and the growth of the church. As such, leaders should be adequately prepared to set a direction for the organizations they are charged with if they hope to encourage ongoing growth.

Theoretical Framework

Contingency theory of leadership is important because it focuses on variables that best suit a specific environment. Accordingly, contingency theory determines the style of leadership that should be adopted when leading a particular environment. White and Hodgson who researched contingency theories argue that effective leadership is not entirely about qualities of leadership but about striking a correct balance between the needs, behaviors and context. Good leaders have the ability to assess the needs of their followers, take stock of the situation at hand and adjust their behaviors and qualities in order to achieve the established vision, mission, goals and objectives. According to the theory, success in any organization depends on leadership style, aspects of the situation and the behavior of the followers. For effective church growth and maturity it is essential for the church leader to develop qualities which are appropriate for the situation (Costen, 2007). Accordingly, church institutions can be difficult to lead when a leader has not adopted the right leadership qualities. In a church setting, there are many people who have varied needs and without effective leadership qualities one might not understand those needs and challenges. Therefore, evaluating a particular situation from a contingency point of view is beneficial to the church leader and the growth of the church (Langley & Kahnweiler, 2003). Because contingency theory applies to a particular environment, it provides a crucial opportunity for leaders to easily achieve the objectives of the church.

Contingency theory is very important in leadership as it enables those leading others to develop leadership qualities based on the situation. When it comes to church growth and development, the leader ought to develop qualities to lead the congregation towards growing the church. Through contingency theory the leader would be in a position to understand the environment and ensure that all the members of the church are brought on board while working towards building a church. Many churches that have successfully grown have embraced the principles of contingency theory (Yancey, 2009). The principles of contingency theory and leadership enable the pastor to help the congregation better understand the requirements of growing a church. Therefore, the pastor has to be a visionary leader and able to manage and predict the behavior of all those who are involved in growing the church.

Principles of contingency theory involve everyone in decision-making and thus ensure that all are involved in spreading the gospel in communities that have not accessed or even understood the word of God. While spreading the word of God, the pastors and the members of the church work together. Thus, the church leader should develop qualities that enable him or her to effectively lead the congregation.

Contingency theory tasks the pastor to motivate his team and, at the same time, develop relationships. When a leader becomes task motivated he or she will accomplish the task through interpersonal relationships. According to Fielder, the leader's style is determined by how the leader relates to his or her congregation. When the leader has relationships with the members of the congregation, it becomes easy for him or her to accomplish the set goals and objectives (Garrison, 1999, P. 65). A church leader should relate well with the congregation and thus lead them towards accomplishing particular church goals and objectives. For example, through contingency theory a church leader can adopt leader-member relations that create an atmosphere of trust. Furthermore, the congregation will develop loyalty and confidence in the leader. Church leaders who have a vision provide direction and guidance, which are beneficial for church growth and develop. With vision, it is crucial for church leaders to understand favorable conditions that produce growth and expansion of the church.

CHAPTER THREE: RESEARCH DESIGN

Introduction

Research is important because it aids visionary leaders when making decisions. Therefore, it is essential to collect sufficient information pertaining to leadership and church growth. Through information leaders can understand the factors that produce success or failure when planting churches. Furthermore, through the analysis of data a leader can know what should be done to avert failure.

Data Types and Sources

The data collected in this research came from primary and secondary sources. The primary sources were collected from churches that have grown successfully. Through this study the factors relating to success will be understood. It was essential to research leadership styles that have been adopted by leaders of successful churches. It was important to undertake research of the books and journals that have been written by different scholars in America. Furthermore, comparisons will be undertaken regarding the successful churches and those which have failed.

The research analyzes data that has already been collected by other researchers about the subject of visionary leadership. The information that will be gained through analyzing other researcher's work will be of great significance as it will provide an understanding of the most appropriate leadership qualities that can be adopted in the contemporary Christian setting (Wright, & Wright, 1997, P.69). The primary sources of information are crucial for this research. It provides unused, fresh data which can be utilized in determining the kind of leadership qualities necessary for spiritual leaders.

Data Collection Methods

The research applied both qualitative and quantitative methods to gather data. The qualitative research methods that will be applied were highly detailed and thus used to explain the relationship between visionary leadership and the success of church plants.

Different methods were applied to collect and analyze data. One method used to collect primary information was questionnaires. A set of questionnaires were supplied to randomly selected Christian churches in the United States of America through email. The questionnaire could be answered by the members of those churches or the spiritual leaders. It was important to use questionnaires as a method to interact indirectly with the members and leaders of varied churches (Gore, 2013). Thus, through questionnaires crucial information about the church's relationship with its leadership that produced factors resulting in the success or failures of churches were revealed (Wofford, 1999, P.77).

Another important method was the focus group. The focus group method enabled collection of information from different groups who had information about the factors that resulted in either success or failure of the churches. Furthermore, different sources of information collected by various scholars were analyzed to further understand leadership and church growth.

CHAPTER FOUR: SUMMARY OF RESULTS

Introduction

Since the outpouring of Holy Spirit at Pentecost church growth has taken place in various forms. Ideally, it has been the central focus of Christian missions. For instance, the majority of churches that have grown are linked to proper church leadership. Furthermore, revivals have been the strategies used by different leaders to ensure effective growth and expansion. For churches to realize growth spiritual and biblical messages should be utilized. For instance, church leaders should teach members the importance of worshiping together especially when they are planting a church (Patzia, 2001, P.91).

The work of the Holy Spirit is crucial in church planting and growth since time immemorial. Historically, believers have planted, nurtured and ensured church growth through continuous prayer. Leadership is one aspect that directs others towards accomplishing particular assigned duties and responsibilities as a team. By being a leader, one helps himself and others to engage in doing the right thing through the guidance of the Holy Spirit.

The planting, growth, and expansion of the church requires proper leadership to provide spiritual direction. A church leader must have an inspiring vision, set the direction, and offer something new. Church leadership should map out the direction for the growth and expansion of the church. It is of great significance to utilize management and leadership skills to guide the team successfully and effectively accomplish particular goals. Leadership differs according to the individual and the task that needs to be accomplished. Leadership may relate to such aspects as political leadership, religious leadership and campaigning group leadership (Chant, 2012b, p. 77).

As a leader, it is of great significance to show visionary capabilities in order to bring change to society and to those who are being led. Through visionary church leadership the way of doing things in the church will be improved and thus the performance of the company or any other group would be significantly improved. Church leadership involves motivating the team members towards undertaking their assigned duties as required and following biblical teachings that change them spiritually. Thus, as a leader, one should set goals and objectives and inspire the team towards attaining them.

Such a leader can utilize their influence as a motivation for the team members. However, after setting goals and objectives and directing the team members towards them, the leader should monitor the performance of the team and address problems that might hinder the attainment of such goals and objectives (Messner, 2003, P.24). In addition, good leaders do everything necessary to ensure the productivity of the team. Church leaders should lay down groundwork for church members to follow and successfully build a living church.

Vision involves viewing the church or an organization in a diverse lens. It is essential to know where the church is going and ensure the goals and objectives are achieved holistically. A spiritual leader needs passion, strength of will and knowledge to attain long-term goals and objectives. A church leader should inspire the team to attain spiritual goals and objectives. Therefore, the leader ought to be an example in discipline and creativity.

Research reveals that vision is equivalent to destination and seeks to achieve action. However, a balance between vision and action is crucial during church growth as it provides an opportunity for all members to participate in growing and expanding the church. Emphasizing of the church's vision, mission and objectives enables sufficient motivation to the members. Church leaders should have a good understanding of their team. Understanding the team enables the leader to know the things that motivates them and thus they can grow the church together.

The research determined the types of leadership and their importance in church growth and development. Research of successful churches revealed the significance of leadership. Thus, church leaders should know the types of leadership styles which are crucial during the planting, growth and expansion of the church. The research also found that a visionary church leader can develop additional leadership styles. Leadership is the way people use power over others. The best leadership style depends upon the leaders function. Leadership styles can either affect the company positively or negatively. I have covered below, several styles and their impact on an organization's management.

Types and Styles of Leadership

There is never a one-sized-fits-all during management of a particular organization. All organizations operate on different platforms. A church is an important organization, which ensures that members grow together spiritually. Visionary church leaders should adopt and apply certain traits that enable them to lead the congregation successfully. Church leaders can thus apply the following leadership styles as they undertake church leadership roles and activities. These styles of leadership are crucial in growing a church as opposed to other styles of leadership.

Transformational Leadership

Transformational leadership is an important leadership style that has been adopted by different managers and leaders in various situations. People who utilized transformational leadership, in most cases, inspire staff through efficient and effective communication. Furthermore, it is through transformational leadership that spiritual leaders can effectively create desirable environments to encourage participation by all the members of the church. The environment created by transformational leaders is important in that it provides intellectual simulation to church leaders. A transformational leader can adopt various leadership principles during church planting, growth and expansion.

Principles of leadership are crucial in the management of organizations. Through adopting principles of leadership, church leaders can ensure growth and expansion of the planted churches. There are different principles of leadership that can be adopted by pastors and spiritual leaders. Church leaders should understand that leadership is behavior and not a position. To ensure effective growth church leaders should adopt good behavior which is founded on the Christian faith. Leaders are responsible for making decisions on how to plant, grow and expand the church. The dictates of Christian behavior enable leaders to understand the challenges facing their church and thus the leader will eventually take the necessary steps in addressing those challenges.

Another principle is leading by example. According to varied research each leader aims to bring out the best in their team to plant, grow and expand a church.
Therefore, excellent orientation towards church growth and leadership is paramount. Leaders should ensure that members are acquainted with the church's vison. It is crucial for the leader to show church members what to do as well as instruct them. Therefore, leaders should practice what they preach so church members can copy them.
Understanding that leading makes an impact is another important leadership principle. Leaders should learn from previous leaders who have made a positive impact on society. Leadership means setting goals regarding church growth and directing other church members to make an impact on society.

A transformational leader is committed and thus, he or she can confidently spread the gospel and spiritual teaching among the congregation. A committed leader can thus communicate the biblical and spiritual messages to church members more easily. According to research when church members have received spiritual messages more effectively, then they will respond to what the leader is teaching them to do. A transformational leader depends on direction from God in leading the church. Furthermore, a visionary leader is committed to teaching the authority of the Bible and thus can significantly enlarge the congregation.

Democratic leadership

Another style of leadership that can be adopted by a visionary leader is the democratic style of leadership. With the democratic style of leadership, the leader makes decisions based on the input of each team member even though he or she makes consultations with the stakeholders before making any decisions. Democratic leadership has been viewed as the most effective leadership style as it enables the members of the church to make sound decisions. It is also known as the participative leadership or even shared leadership as the members of the team participate actively in organizational roles. It is a type of leadership that can apply to any organization. With this type of leadership, everyone is given an opportunity to participate and provide ideas on how the institution ought to be run. Democratic leadership is very important in growing a church because it treats church members with equality. When church members are challenged to decide how to run the church effectively they develop and grow. A democratic leader offers guidance as they make decisions together. Research proves spiritual leaders who adopt democratic styles of leadership effectively produce greater results.

Churches in the United States of America that have adopted democratic styles of leadership have grown because their leaders create unity as they encourage members to share ideas and opinions. A spiritual leader who is democratic enables members to feel more engaged. According to research the Church of Christ and the United Methodist Church in the United States of America have adopted democratic styles of leadership and their churches have significantly grown. Their strong democratic leadership inspires trust and respect among their followers. More importantly, the churches are sincere and they base their decisions on values and morals which encourage members to achieve significant church growth. Therefore, followers become inspired and take action that contributes to effective church growth. Democratic leadership styles do not fear diverse opinions.

Followers tend to be inspired and respect the leader (Johnson, 1989). More importantly, church members are more committed and involved resulting in more creative solutions to problems in the church (Malphurs, 2004).

Autocratic Leadership

In autocratic leadership all authority lies in one person. Most autocratic leaders are inexperienced and rarely consider suggestions from juniors. A significant percentage of people don't support autocratic leadership. This type of leadership can lead to high turnover and a lot of absenteeism. It also suppresses creativity because strategies are determined by a single person.

Bureaucratic Leadership

Bureaucratic leaders depend on policies to fulfill organizational goals. This type of leader depends on procedures and processes instead of people. A risk that may arise from this style of leadership is resistance or disinterest which leads to the frustration of desired results. Bureaucratic leadership lacks maturity and has little impact on developing people. Democratic leaders allow participation of others before a decision is made. This leads to job satisfaction from workers and lots of creativity because the communication is upward and downward and thus is the most preferred leadership because of fairness, courage, competence, and honesty (Conn, 1997). However, this leadership style's weakness is giving equal shared stakes in the outcome as well as the level of expertise, and the decision making process is slow.

Transactional Leadership

Transactional leaders compensate followers with a promotion, new responsibilities or a change in duties. However, this kind of leadership creates expectations (Cheetham, 2000). This leads to risks when production is low and there is nothing to give in return resulting in a low output. Also punishing bad practices inhibits the employee's creative potential.

Here an environment with intellectual stimulation is created. There's a total change initiated in the organization, groups, and individuals as well as others. Leaders set many challenging expectations thus achieving higher performance. Leaders thus empower their followers with knowledge, expertise, and vision that changes those they lead thus leading to the best leadership outcome in an organization (Getz et al., 2000). It's best suited for quick paced and dynamic environments which need creative problem solving and commitment.

Laissez-faire Leadership

Employees are free to do the best they can when leadership adopts a laissez-faire method. It's best practiced by leaders in organizations where people are more experienced resulting in high production. However, it needs total monitoring and effective communication to prevent slipping of work standards.

Coaching Leadership

Leaders teach and supervise their followers. These types of leaders can be highly operational in settings where outcome requires improvement. Followers are aided in improving their skills. This type of leadership encourages motivation and inspiration among followers. This makes the followers feel appreciated and involved thus working hard with one spirit leads to improved organizational performance.

Some prefer one kind of leadership over others. A leader must know how to balance between different environments, people, and groups. Leaders must use their knowledge and expertise to identify the kind of environment they control to enable them to apply strategic decisions and know the best leadership style to run their organizations well.

Visionary Leaders and Church Growth

Visionary leaders are the significant agents for growing a church. A visionary leader understands where the church started and when it needs to be in the future.

Vision in a church requires an individual to formulate significant strategies that are crucial in taking the spiritual institution to a different level. Establishing and sustaining a vision for an organization calls for creativity and discipline. A spiritual leader should have the strength of will and necessary knowledge which are important in achieving long-term goals.

According to research, a visionary leader is a focused individual able to inspire the congregation to reach organizational goals and attain a well, coordinated spiritual nourishment for everyone (Kirby, 2014). A church's vision equates to the destination in which members would like to reach within a short period. Emphasizing the vision provides motivation.

Visionary leaders are the builders of a new dawn. They are important in every situation because they offer solutions to challenges that call for effective leadership. In Christianity and church growth leaders work with the power of intentionality and alignment with a higher purpose of ensuring members of the church become spiritually mature. Their eyes are set on the horizon of spiritual growth and fulfillment. Because they are prayerful, they view the big picture of the overall church, challenges facing the church, and how well they can handle those challenges through spiritual means. Pastors and or spiritual leaders dream about building an important church that offers solutions to spiritual problems people face. A visionary leader is not only good with words but he or she also acts. Visionary leaders enable church members to spiritual transformation. When planting a church, visionary leaders normally decide what the church intends to bring to the environment where it has been established. Another important factor that leads to church or community growth and development spiritually is the focus on biblical teaching. The most relevant way of moving people from the church or the community forward is through engaging in biblical teaching (Barnard, 1993, P.145). Visionary leaders engage in spiritual and biblical teachings. It is always important for the church or spiritual community leaders to ensure regular biblical teachings to realize expansion and provide spiritual needs to the members. As a leader, it is significant to engage the church and the Christian community in Bible study and encourage them to study on their own.

For spiritual church growth it is also important to clarify the role of the church and the Christian communities. People should be encouraged to mature in their beliefs and embrace personal development practices as part of their spiritual journey. Members should understand that being part of a community of believers includes encouraging each other towards spiritual growth and development, so they can grow the church together (Van Gelder, 2000). A spiritual leader ought to encourage the congregation to reflect on spiritual scriptures and biblical teachings.

A visionary leader that aspires to grow and reach spiritual maturity focuses on missions. Growing churches involve establishing missions that spread the word of God. As the word traverses through different regions spiritual development is encouraged, which provides opportunities for spiritual growth and stability. Churches that do not focus on mission establishment have stagnated. Therefore, it is essential for pastors and spiritual leaders to realize the importance of Christian missions and thus establish them in their communities and other regions (Fletcher, 2006, P.47). Leaders should also create a vision for the church and missions, which encourage members to become involved in nurturing the church.

Every leader who is visionary begins by following someone else's vision that gives him a blueprint of what is expected. According to research, the fundamental of visionary practice is to enable the leader to develop the abilities of others and achieve the vision. Therefore, a future visionary leader submits to authority that comes from God. A visionary leader is shaped by the strengths and limitations which are crucial in the vision and vision development. Visionary leaders are significantly very important in growing a church plant (Erickson, 1998). Visionary leaders have a compelling vision for their organizations. These leaders can see beyond the challenges and the ambiguities of the present, and inspire and empower the leaders of today and tomorrow. Visionary leaders are important to ensure team members are provided with ample opportunity to work towards realizing the vision and mission of the church. Therefore, the church leader charts how to develop a course for the church and implements that course. Visionary leaders in the church do not control the members of the church but guide them to work together in order to achieve spiritual nourishment and expand their spiritual services to areas untouched by the word of God. More importantly, visionary leaders provide freedom for members of the church to determine the best path to realize the vision.

Moreover, visionary leaders who would like to develop the church should have good communications with church members that live in a world of endless distractions. Effective collaborations are important to create something that will expand to areas which have not been reached with the word of God.

Church leaders should be inspirational by nature. Inspirational leaders enable other leaders to tap into new emotions. They ignite the passion of church members and drive their emotions in the right direction to bring out the best in building an inclusive church. For a church to grow and expand effectively its leaders need to be emotionally intelligent. Such leaders inspire consistency among other leaders and insure they take advantage of opportunity in areas which have not received or have not heard about God's word. In addition, a visionary leader ought to be open-minded. Such leaders see the big picture and are flexible when planning the course of church growth based on the opinions provided by church members.

Principles of Visionary Leadership

Principles of good leadership are important to manage any organization. Accordingly, when church leaders adopt good principles, they will be in a position to grow and expanded the church. There are many principles of leadership which can be adopted to ensure the church has significant growth. According to research effective leadership is very important. When good principles of leadership are adopted it makes it very simple to grow church plants. It is important for a spiritual leader such as a pastor to adopt a unique formula of success and thus become an authentic leader who can lead the congregation to solutions for pertinent problems.

Through adoption of principles of leadership, church leaders will be in the position to ensure growth and expansion of the church. There are different principles of leadership that can be adopted by pastors and spiritual leaders. Church leaders should understand that leadership is behavior and not a position. To ensure the effective growth of the church, pastors and other church leadership should adopt good behavior which is founded on Christian faith. Church leaders are responsible for making decisions on how to plant, grow and expand the church. Through Christian behavior, leaders will be in a position to understand the challenges facing their church and thus will eventually take the necessary steps in addressing those challenges (Leithwood, & Jantzi, 2005, P.128).

Another principle of good leadership is to lead by example. According to various research each leader strives to get the best from their team. In this context church leaders want to get the best from their team in planting, growing and expanding a church.

Therefore, excellent orientation towards church growth and leadership is paramount. Leaders should make sure that all members get acquainted with the church's vison. It is crucial for the leader to show church members what to do rather than telling them what to do (Fletcher, 2006, P.89). Therefore, if leaders practice what they preach the church members will imitate them.

Another important leadership principle to understand that leading means making an impact. Leaders should follow the example of previous leaders who have made an impact on society. Church leaders should also learn from other leaders who have a positive impact on society. Leadership means setting goals regarding church growth and directing other church members towards achieving those goals and objectives. Leadership is the art of leading others towards achieving particular goals and objectives. One of the significant goals of the Christian church is to prepare God's people towards achieving spiritual goals and objectives. The quality of interpersonal and communication is significant with regards to the pastoral care. In most churches, it is impossible to understand everyone intimately, but through effective communication, a pastor will be in the position to know what the members of the church are going through. Good communications are crucial for building trust. When Jesus taught the people, he maintains that leaders ought to understand the congregation through constant communications with them. Even though every church has the formal leadership, it is also important to have informal leaders who will ensure effective communication of the message.

Research shows that an effective leader is an individual with a passion for a cause which is bigger than they are. A pastor with a vision and dream will better the church by ensuring effective delivery of the pastoral message to the congregation. Furthermore, an effective leader should be charismatic and ready to assist others when they have problems. According to research done by (Clebsch & Jaekle, 1994), an effective pastor is the one that is courageous ready to make difficult decisions and carry the assign duties more diligently. Furthermore, the authors argue that leadership implies values which are life-giving to the church and the society. Pastoral values are embedded in respect for improving the lives of other people. As a leader, a pastor should show respect towards other people.

As a pastor, it is crucial to have effective leadership qualities which include listening openly to all the members. When pastors do not listen to the members of the church, they may end up with a poor relationship with them and therefore develop negative attitudes towards him. Thus, it is crucial for the pastor to offer and accept constructive suggestions. Giving clear directions also makes a pastor an effective leader. That will involve providing formal and informal presentations that enable them to identify and solve problems. As a pastor, it is also significant to set the desired behavior by showing appreciation towards others' contributions.

Every pastor regardless of how the size of the church will find the congressional needs never-ending. There is no time when each of the church member's needs is fully met. It is important for the church leader to understand that to ensure the provision of good care to all the church members. When the pastor understand that, he or she will be in the position to develop a plan to serve the members well. Research has shown that one of the most common reasons that result in pastoral mistakes is the failure of the pastor to understand the significance of the size of the church (Berkley, 2008). Decisions are made based on the church size and the culture binding the members of such a church. As a leader, it is important for the pastor to understand such a culture to make good decisions and minister well to all the members of the church. The paper is important because it examines the dynamics of leadership and pastoral care and its implication in the contemporary church settings.

Nurturing is one of the most significant roles of a pastor since the church is currently experiencing an influx of a high number of membership rate. Therefore, the pastor's role as a primary caregiver is viewed as inadequate to meet the spiritual needs of each church member. Accordingly, it is important for the church leader to understand and adopt different pastoral and nurturing models to meets the changing needs of the contemporary church setting (Carter, 2009). An equipping model is the most significant nurturing model that can be adopted to ensure that all the members have been provided with the right information which eventually sees them grow spiritually.

Research shows that pastoral care has many dimensions. It flows from the identification and example of Jesus as the Shepherd of God. However, it means that it can be extended through the members of the church and the ministry. Those pastors who engage in the "pastoral care" are never using the gifts of the people and the churches but are developing the body of believers. The law of Christ is fulfilled by the pastor through the carrying of each other's burdens. The church through their leader is called to care for the persons in need. The faith communities and the leaders have to show an open and honest community. Research has shown that North American pastors and congregations typically encourage their members to seek medical treatments for those who physically ill. It is an important activity for the church, and the leader should know how to deal with such issues. Pastors being the church leaders refer to members to the centers of treatments, counselors and also the recognized twelve-step programs for spiritual and psychosocial problems (Carter, 2009). It is, therefore, important that the leader understand the needs of every member to provide them with the pastoral care that improves their living standards.

An effective leader engages in a periodical assessment of his or her performance. It is important for a pastor to take periodical stock of their strengths and also the shortcomings. Effective leaders ask themselves questions like "What am I good in? What do I like to do? What are my greatest strengths and weaknesses? When a pastor understands his or her greatest strengths and weaknesses, it makes him or her a good decision maker. Research shows that understanding one's areas of weaknesses does not make such an individual weak but enables them to delegate to others who have such abilities to undertake them and eventually achieve the desire goals and objectives. A pastor should not cling to the false belief that they can do it all. However, he or she should seek for members of the church who can undertake some particular activities efficiently for achieving desired goals and objectives. As a pastor, it is necessary to continuously work on the weak areas (de Matviuk, 2002). That will enable the pastor to deliver a quality pastoral message to the congregation that positively changes their lives. Through continuous improvement of one's weaknesses, a pastor would be in the position to get more members and thus enlarge the church. Therefore, message delivery to the members of the church will be enhanced as the pastor will have improved his or her spiritual knowledge.

Furthermore, having positive perception towards the church and the members of the church will also make a pastor an effective leader. Positive perception is important to the pastor because it makes him or she efficiently understands the needs of the congregation. Some members of the church value trust than from their leaders. Therefore, being a trustworthy leader will enable the pastor to discharge his or her duties in a more effective manner. Furthermore, it is important for the leader to understand leadership is about people. A church leader should understand the challenges being faced by church members and make sure their problems have been accorded with appropriate solutions.

Therefore, unity among the church members and the leadership of the church ought to be embraced in order to realize effective leadership (Langley & Kahnweiler, 2003). Another essential of good leadership involves motivating team members to undertake their assigned duties and follow biblical teachings that change them spiritually. Thus, as a leader, one should set goals and objectives and inspire the team to attain them. Such a leader can utilize their emotional influence as a motivation. However, after setting goals and objectives and directing the team members towards them, the leader should monitor the performance of the team and address the problems that might hinder the attainment of such goals and objectives (Wong, Davey, & Church, 2007, P.77). In addition, good leaders must ensure the productivity of the team is encouraged. Leaders should lay down groundwork for church members to follow and successfully build a living church.

In contemporary church ministry, theology and belief directly concern the individual believer and provide a basis for assurance of salvation, which in turn allows church growth and expansion. Fundamental issues relating to the deity of Christ, the work of redemption and the experience of divine grace are undertaken through contemporary theology by ordained leaders. It provides the standards absolute righteousness are crucial for Christian relationship and engaging in other good things. The Bible is a crucial tool that teaches how God relates to humanity and how he rules creation and thus should be embraced by church leaders.

Therefore, by spreading Christianity people will understand the existence of God. God's authority over creation demonstrates that God is the only Supreme Being and people should believe in him. When an individual understands and believes in God he or she receives an assurance of salvation.

In Christianity revival involves bringing non-believers back to life. Revival is a biblical concept that ensures the growth of the church through bringing more members to the already established church or to the newly planted church. Revival is crucial in the planting of a church as it makes new members of the church strong through biblical interpretations. Revival restores churches to good conditions and new life (Chant, 2013). In revival the Holy Spirit draws people closer to God. The majority of churches in contemporary society are filled with non-committed Christians who attend church services without being serious about the word of God. Some do not understand what the Bible advocates. Therefore, revival is a crucial aspect of church growth and expansion as it enables biblical understanding by church members. Whenever the love of God's people has grown cold revival is required.

Churches need a renewal to ensure those who lack understanding will become spiritually conscious. Revival leads people into spiritual realities and prompts them to examine themselves and their faith. It is through revival that Christian believers acknowledge God and continuously engage in a prayer that produces church grow and expansion. Personal revival returns the individual to a right relationship with God and encourages them to achieve God's purposes. Personal revival enables members of the church to do the work which was ordained by God and thus they will win the hearts of those who have not turned to God (McCoy, 2005). Through revival missions Christians embrace biblical authority that makes them strong and able to achieve what God desires them to achieve. Revival is an opportunity for believers to renew their faith. The Bible teaches that all of humanity is prone to making mistakes. Therefore, Christians might make mistakes that hinder other people from joining the church. In such cases, the growth and expansion of the church is negatively impacted. Revival is a way to teach believers in newly planted churches the importance of resolving internal conflicts peacefully. Resolving conflicts peacefully ensures a unity and thwarts differences that might have caused the church to shatter at a tender stage.

Christians desire to see their churches grow, expand and meet the needs of their members. Scholars have argued that growing a church is biblical and God ordains it. The revival of churches that have not been growing very fast has become the norm in contemporary society. Theologians take into account the principles of planting and

39

nurturing the growth of the church. The American way of life has been a cultural aspect of planting and nurturing churches by missionaries (Hesselgrave, 1980). They have planted churches in various countries through the adoption of cultural values. Therefore, the current churches in African countries were built with the assistance of American culture because the missionaries were mostly from America. Christians need to realize that culture works immensely in the planting and nurturing of the church. Evangelism or the evangelical Christianity refers to a worldwide, trans-denominational movement which maintains that the essential of the Gospel have such important aspects as the salvation by grace. Accordingly, the salvation by Grace in theology is achieved by having faith in the atonement of Jesus Christ. Research shows that evangelicals and theologians believe in the centrality of the conversion. Therefore, evangelists engage in spreading the Christian word to all the regions of the world through the evangelical movements. Evangelicalism has been regarded as the most dynamic religious movement in the contemporary society. The developing countries have embraced the evangelical movements, and thus such countries have seen registered the fastest growing Christianity (Johnston, 2009). The evangelical movement is very crucial in spreading the Gospel by teaching people about the life, death, and resurrection of Jesus Christ. In contemporary evangelism series of revivals are conducted through missionary works spreading the Gospel of Jesus Christ.

Evangelical theology is significant because it provides people an opportunity to be "born again." The central message of evangelical theology is to ensure justification by faith in Christ and repentance by the believers. Through evangelical theology, people are encouraged to turn away from the sin. It is through an evangelical theology that Christians are assured salvation. The evangelical theologians have embraced the aspect of Biblicism to teach people the existence of biblical authority. Such provides an opportunity for biblical inspiration and how biblical teachings offers an opportunity to the members to repent to attain salvation (Johnston, 2009).

Evangelism is also very important because it ensures that people from diverse backgrounds live together as a community of believers. The development of Christian ministries has been motivated by the evangelical teachings conducted by those who are born again. Through the teachings, people get to understand the significance of being born again and offering also engaging in evangelical movements with others who are born again.

It is through the evangelical theology that people get to understand the reality of the world. Because theologians move from one area to another teaching about the Christian believes, the power of the church is being spread from a region to another (Pinnock, 2001). For example, research shows that early evangelical missionary theology taught reality the reality of good and bad spirits. Furthermore, the theologians teach about the power of Jesus to defeat the evil spirit in the current world. Through such the word of God is spread and thus it is felt through various regions. That, in turn, increases the number of Christians improving the community of believers

The most complex problems which are encountered by theologians when planting new churches in different regions can be addressed through revival. Many churches have shut their doors because of poor commitment from members and church leaders. Such requires more revival missions to encourage the importance of growing a church to improve their lives and the community they live in.

Even though America has many churches more need to be planted because of the growth in population (Ratliff & Cox, 1993). Additionally, the current and projected growth rate in population in other regions of the world indicates there is a high demand for planting more churches to cater to the needs of people. Through revival missions pastors and church leaders can teach the significance of planting new churches in different regions. The aspects of revival and church planting which the pastor can teach the congregation include training, discipleship and encouraging new members to be committed. When the church leader or the pastor equips or trains the members to be committed, the church will grow and expand very fast. Pastors should encourage revival missions in areas where there are few churches.

Understanding and Solving Challenges

Another important theme is leaders who understand and solve challenges facing church growth. Defining leadership in any organization immediately raises questions regarding the mission, vision, and objectives. As a leader, it is crucial to understand what church planting is all about to ensure well-coordinated efforts between church leadership and the congregation. The leader, such as the pastor or any spiritual leader, ought to use prayer and biblical messages to solve problems. Through prayer God will provide solutions to pertinent issues.

According to the Bible, spiritual people orient everything including their lives to God through continuous prayer (Wagner, 2010, P.44). A spiritual leader builds his life and the church on the word of God and prayer. An effective leader who trusts in the Lord will easily figure out challenges facing the church and acknowledge the presence of the Lord when addressing such problems. Furthermore, God's word is crucial in that it permeates

41

all God does and thinks. Therefore, he does not act with human or worldly wisdom but through the use of scriptures to reveal the hidden challenges facing the church and possible solutions.

Another important way of understanding and solving problems facing a church is for the entire congregation to walk with God daily and practice the reality of the living God. As a leader, it is important to conduct the business of the church in accordance with prayer and scriptures. As a spiritual individual it is also crucial to read books regarding church management and conflict resolution that base their arguments on spiritual wisdom rather than on worldly wisdom. When a church leader reads such books he or she will be equipped to resolve problems with spiritual solutions.

As a leader it is also crucial to understand and appreciate unity and community. Unity is an important way organizations can address challenges. Therefore, as a church leader, it is advisable to engage in continuous monitoring of church members and how they undertake various activities (Leithwood & Jantzi, 2005, P. 332). A church is normally established in a particular community and it is the responsibility of that church to provide solutions to pertinent issues facing a society. God wants the church to reach everyone in the society and offer the best it can offer on a spiritual basis. Furthermore, through continuous prayer and spiritual interpretations a church will be in the position to teach the best way to grow a spiritual church.

According to research, a church leader ought to solve problems pertaining to church growth and leadership. The early church spread rapidly throughout the hostile Roman Empire in the first century through the work of evangelists. They taught believers in the church to follow Jesus Christ and share the freedom of forgiveness that Jesus advocated. In the current society a church planting movement is crucial to ensure the growth and expansion of the church. Planting the church is achieved through evangelical movements by missionaries, theologians, pastors, and believers. A church planting movement is crucial because it wins the hearts of believers. Church planting can result in achievement of one church or a handful of churches in a community.

Church planting and revival is borrowed from the works of the early missionaries. Accordingly, the missionary movement (1800-1900) had a standard of practice that was geared towards building a missionary compound, a missionary station, and missionary church. The planting of the first church encouraged the missionaries to carry on with planting churches until there were several churches in a community. The knowledge of how the first missionaries planted churches is crucial to contemporary believers because it enables them to plant churches too. The recent contemporary theology shows interfaith dialogue is very crucial to the Christian world as it ensures peaceful coexistence among all the believers. Evangelical theology is significant because it provides people an opportunity to be "born again." The central message of evangelical theology is to ensure justification by faith in Christ and repentance by the believers. Through evangelical theology, people are encouraged to turn away from the sin. It is through an evangelical theology that Christians are assured salvation. The evangelical theologians have embraced the aspect of Biblicism to teach people the existence of biblical authority (Williams, 2000). Such provides an opportunity for biblical inspiration and how biblical teachings offer an opportunity to the members to repent to attain salvation. It is through the evangelical theology that people get to understand the reality of the world. Because theologians move from one area to another teaching about the Christian believes, the power of the church is being spread from a region to another (Elwell, 2001). For example, research shows that early evangelical missionary theology taught reality the reality of good and bad spirits. Furthermore, the theologians teach about the power of Jesus to defeat the evil spirit in the current world. Through such the word of God is spread and thus it is felt through various regions. That, in turn, increases the number of Christians improving the community of believers.

Furthermore, it provides an understanding of the challenges that are faced by evangelical theologians and how those challenges can be addressed. For example, Lightner (1995) explains God's existence. Therefore, it is the resource that one will be in the position to understand how the existence of God in crucial for the Christian growth. The book has information that creates a relationship between a Christian and God. The Christian Gospel is spread through the resource, and many people can be converted to Christianity (Freddoso, 1998). Being a popular movement, evangelism emphasizes on being born again and providing a personal relationship between the Christians and Jesus Christ. Through the evangelical theology, evangelists engage in teaching and describing the evangelical approach to the Christian faith. Many scholars argue that evangelical theology commits a high scripture. Accordingly, the Bible is the sole authority for practice and faith in the life of the Christians.

The indigenous policy of planting churches began in the mid-nineteenth century when missionaries and other believers agreed that young churches should be self-propagating, self- governing and self-supporting. Therefore, the skill of planting and developing churches was extracted from these early principles that produced many converts. Evangelical methods were also important in developing the church and ensuring that the number of believers increased. The culture of the communities should be adopted to enable the church to grow. Many churches have failed to grow because of the poor mainstreaming of the local community's cultural values. Evangelical movements ought to take into consideration the cultural values of the society to ensure future growth of churches (Church Growth International, 2009). More importantly, future growth depends on the Bible translation used. Leaders have to teach members the significance of building a good relationship with Jesus Christ. They have to teach people what Jesus requires them and to follow the Bible's teachings. That will enable the congregation to follow God's commandments faithfully resulting in church growth. A new church ought to engage in preaching, biblical worship and pursuing an understanding of gospel.

Most churches in contemporary society need to experienced revival. Revival is crucial because it ensures a spiritual awakening from the state of stagnation in life of a believer. Revival restores a love for God and appreciation of God's holiness. Additionally, it ensures that believers have a passion for the word of God and the church. When believers have a passion for God and the church growth is possible. Revival is also essential in that it invigorates and sometimes deepens the faith of believers and opens their eyes to see the reality of God in society (Meyers, 2003). Thus, believers make new beginnings in their lives and eventually achieve church growth and expansion. Revival also generates the power to live peacefully in a righteous world.

Importance of Visionary Leadership in Church Planting

Church planting is crucial to establishing new churches in communities. These churches should function independently. A spiritual leader understands the purpose of church growth is to enrich the society with the word of God. It also needs to stay in relationship with the denomination to develop a network that works together to expand the church. Historically, the concept of church planting has taken place for nearly twenty centuries. Christianity spread to other areas when church planting and nurturing were embraced.

The church is crucial because it address the social and spiritual needs of society. For example, churches provide an opportunity for people to learn what is going on in different cultural communities. The planting of churches in different societies is also crucial to teach people regarding peace and living in unity as a community. More importantly churches provide the social needs of society (Brown, 1979). For example, many churches provide support to the poor. A church leader should also understand that Evangelicalism refers to a worldwide, trans-denominational movement which maintains that the essential of the Gospel is salvation by grace. Accordingly, salvation by grace is achieved by faith in the atonement of Jesus Christ. The task of a pastor involves not just the communication of biblical truth but understanding the totality of the congregation. If the pastor does not have an understanding of the combination of all the members of the church, then he will find himself or herself in a myriad of criticism and problems. The knowledge and skills of leadership are crucial to the pastor because it provides him or her with the opportunity to effectively organize a team. According to Cowen (2003), leadership within the church should be understood from an organizational standpoint. Leadership involves guiding the members of a church towards achieving common goals and objectives. However, biblical leadership is much more than the organizational leadership. Cowen (2003) defines that pastoring is more spiritual but not organizational. A pastor should have the ability to influence others towards understanding the existence of God. Furthermore, a pastor will have to guide the congregation towards achieving the right discipleship growth. A pastor has to understand spiritual requirements of the church members and place emphasis on the spiritual transformation. Pastoral care is intentional in that is pastor ought not to sit back and be a passive leader but should spiritually guide the members towards a spiritual nourishment (Berkley, 2008).

Furthermore, the pastor is supposed to understand the dynamics of the church size. Research shows that smaller churches function differently from larger churches. Because the smaller churches and the larger churches have varied needs and requirements, the leadership of the two churches should be understood differently. Therefore, leadership as a pastor is forcing a particular model on the members of the congregation (Fowler, 2008). In any time of the church, leadership is crucial for the well-being and the health of the congregation. The pastor should understand that the Christ if the ultimate leader of the church and he or she should seek for the guidance to from the Christ to effective and successful lead the members of the church.

Research shows that evangelicals and theologians believe in the centrality of the conversion. Therefore, evangelists engage in spreading the gospel to all regions of the world through the evangelical movement. Evangelicalism has been regarded as the most dynamic religious movement in contemporary society. Developing countries that have embraced the evangelical movement register the fastest growth of Christianity (Johnston, 2009). The evangelical movement has been crucial in spreading the gospel by teaching people about the life, death, and resurrection of Jesus Christ. In contemporary evangelism a series of revivals are conducted through missionaries to spread the Gospel of Jesus Christ.

Evangelical theology is significant because it provides people the opportunity to be "born again." The central message of evangelical theology is to ensure justification by faith in Christ and repentance by the believers. Through evangelical theology people are encouraged to turn away from sin. It is through an evangelical theology that Christians are assured of salvation.

Evangelical theologians teach people about biblical authority. Such provides an opportunity for biblical inspiration and how biblical teachings offer an opportunity for people to repent and receive salvation (Johnston, 2009).

Evangelism is also important to ensure people from diverse backgrounds live together as a community of believers. The development of Christian ministries is the result of evangelical teachings by those who are born again. Through these teachings people understand the significance of being born again and engaging in evangelical movements with others who are born again.

Through evangelical theology people understand the world they live in. Because theologians move from one area to another teaching the Christian believers, the power of the church is spread from a region to another (Pinnock, 2001). For example, research shows that early evangelical missionary theology taught the reality of good and bad spirits. Furthermore, theologians teach about the power of Jesus to defeat evil spirits. Through this teaching the word of God is spread and its power felt in various regions. That, in turn, increases the number of Christians increasing the community of believers.

They have educated less fortunate children who eventually become successful. Additionally, new churches have given hope to people who might be hopeless. For instance, sick people may lose hope believing they will succumb to their disease. However, when church members, pastors and church leaders visit and pray with them and God heals them they gain hope. Therefore, planting new churches in different regions of the world eventually gives hope to the less fortunate that with God everything is possible.

Another importance of visionary leadership and church planting is the fact that it provides biblical messages to the community thus making them spiritually strong. Spiritual growth has been viewed as difficult by those who practice Christianity because they lack biblical teachings. A leader has to be someone who understands the society they live in and provide the necessary support to realize effective church growth. As a leader it is of great significance to have members in agreement and make sure they have mastered the required knowledge to achieve significant spiritual growth. When many churches are planted and prosper in society, it provides greater opportunities for those who desire to live righteously. They will encourage one another spiritually and the church will grow to satisfy their needs. The findings are very crucial with regards to current ministry practice.

The Christian community in the current world has become diverse and requires crucial leadership that provides an opportunity for the church to grow and expand. Research proves visionary leadership offers critical knowledge for addressing challenges facing church planting, growth, and expansion. The Christian community is called into being by God through acts of incarnation, life, death and resurrection of Jesus Christ and the gift of the Holy Spirit (Epes, 1948). The findings acknowledge changes which are found in the current church. Moreover, it is through the findings that current ministry has an opportunity learn how to build and grow a church that depends on the word of God. Church ministries have the responsibility of ensuring that there are many growing churches in the remote areas of countries. Therefore, missionaries can encourage spontaneous growth through continuous prayer.

Church planting is also crucial in that it enables people from different backgrounds to share good news regarding the Gospel and Christian living. It is through the revival and church planting that people share the passion to care for spiritually needy people. Groups and denominations will build peace and cohesive living through revival and planting of new churches in remote areas of the world (Williams, 1994). Church planting is crucial for an evangelist to conduct their mission of saving the spiritually lost.

Church Development and Spiritual Growth

New Christians and spiritual leaders are produced by the church. Empowering the church community to grow spiritually is important to teach members behavior and how to treat each other in a Christian manner. Research has shown that spiritual attainment by the church community is only achieved through empowering leadership. According to Christian research and biblical teachings, God wants the church community to develop and grow spiritually. Growing the church is important because it ensures all people understand the existence of God. Spiritual development and growth of the church are only attained through great leadership. Everything is known to rise or fall due to leadership (Scuderi, 2010). Therefore, spiritual leaders should pray for wisdom to realize growth and development of the churches they lead.

Another important factor that leads to church growth and development spiritually is the focus on biblical teaching. The most relevant way of moving people from the church forward is through biblical teaching. It is always important for the church or spiritual community leaders to ensure regular biblical teachings in the church and in the community. As a pastor, it is significant to engage the church or the Christian community to participate in Bible study and to study on their own.

For spiritual development and growth, it is also important to clarify the role of the church in the Christian community. People should be encouraged to mature in their belief and embrace personal development practices as part of their spiritual journey. They should understand that as a community of believers they need to encourage each other towards spiritual growth and development (Yancey, 2009). A spiritual leader or a pastor needs to encourage the congregation to reflect on scriptures and biblical teachings.

A church or a community that aspires to grow and reach spiritual maturity focuses on missions. Churches grow when missions are established that spread the word of God. As the word traverses through different regions spiritual development is encouraged, so members can attain spiritual growth and stability. Churches that do not focus on mission establishment have stagnated regarding spiritual growth and development. Therefore, it is essential for pastors and spiritual leaders to realize the importance of Christian missions.

Importance of a Pastor in Spiritual Development

A pastor plays a crucial role in the development of the church and the community of believers. Through the pastor a church develops and grows spiritually. The pastor develops the local church in a manner that enables it to grow and have a future generation of believers. A pastor is very significant in spearheading the inception, development and implementation of the activities regarding the church and the community (Baruth, Wilcox, & Saunders, 2013). The mission statement is also crucial to the church. It is, therefore, the role of the pastor to guide the church or the community in developing a mission and vision statement. The mission statement should be informed by biblical teachings, and such is only possible through the efforts of the pastor.

The pastor is also important with regards to equipping members with spiritual messages. In most cases, a pastor provides direction to the members of the church or the community. It is through biblical teachings and spiritual messages that the pastor will inspire the members to work towards ensuring Christian faith.

Furthermore, pastoral care is also administered by the pastor to the community and church development and spiritual growth. Guiding and counseling are part of the processes that ensure spiritual development of the community and the church. However, for the pastor to guide and counsel the members regarding spiritual development, he or she should be in the position to understand their problems.

Congregations need a pastor to grow spiritually, emotionally and numerically. Research shows that people live in a crazy world with many challenges. Therefore, to realize spiritual growth it is crucial for pastors to teach them how to avoid those challenges and live righteous lives.

Furthermore, traditional doctrines should also be passed to the congregation through teaching and preaching by the pastor. Traditions are important for the growth of the church and the community. Caregiving, counseling, visitation, comforting and taking care of the church should be facilitated by the pastor (Van Gelder, 2000). Such provides an opportunity for spiritual understanding by the people to develop and grow.

Leadership is very important as it provides significant knowledge regarding the spiritual development of the pastor, church and the community. Scholars have significantly portrayed the necessity of spiritual growth and development of Christian communities. They have also researched an individual's requirements to attain spiritual growth and development. For example, it is through (Gemignani, 2002) that readers understand that Christian faith is very important in the spiritual development of the church and the society. Many pastors appreciate church members who have faith and believe things which they have not seen. Therefore, the church and the community of believers appreciate the importance of faith in spiritual development and growth.

It is also through the research that scholars offer crucial knowledge about the spiritual growth and development of the pastor. For their message to be effective the pastor or spiritual leader should encourage people to discuss how to grow spiritually. Members of the church or the community should be encouraged to engage in bible studies. It is an important duty of the pastor to ensure availability of materials that encourage spiritual development. A church or a community that aspires to grow and reach spiritual maturity focuses on missions (Von Campenhausen & Campenhausen, 2009). Growing churches involves establishing missions that spread the word of God. As the word traverses through different regions, spiritual development is encouraged that provides an opportunity for the members to attain spiritual growth and stability. Spreading the word of God is the responsibility of church members.

A church can develop a sound philosophy for Christian education through engaging in spirituality development. The Christian education regarding faith development, spiritual development and growth involve people from different levels. A greater effectiveness of the church and the community is realized when all the people encourage spiritual development and growth. Such encourages everyone to realize the existence of God.

Spiritual development is crucial because it ensures a positive personal growth. It is through spiritual development that members of the church are encouraged to love one another. Therefore, as they love each other, they are also showing their love for God. Furthermore, a spiritually developed person recognizes the existence of God as the protector of their lives. Such is applicable in the current church as spiritual growth and development involves increasing knowledge and understanding of God's word (Barna, 2000). The church and community members will be provided with spiritual messages on how to live and lead righteous lives and decrease the engagement in sinful activities. The research provides pastors an opportunity to understand the practical application of spiritual messages to develop and grow the church.

The research provides an individual with knowledge of how previous churches and Christian ministries have grown spiritually. They can then apply such knowledge to develop themselves and enrich the members of the church or the community with the spiritual messages. Contemporary worship is seen by many Christians and Scholars as preferable to the traditional ways of worship. The contemporary worship services have varied strengths and weaknesses especially in the contemporary society where there are different generations with varied needs. The most important strength of the contemporary worship is that it brings together dynamic music, compelling dramas and moving real-life stories. Because the contemporary worship adopts music while worshipping, it therefore, attracts many members compared to traditional worship (Cheetham, 2000, P.66). For instance, the praise and worship songs in contemporary worship is accompanied by an ensemble of songs and instruments consisting of the electronic piano, electric guitar, drum kit and acoustic guitar. Such instruments are utilized to emphasize particular messages. In most cases, the music used in the contemporary churches is upbeat, vibrant and worshipful meaning the congregation can easily understand the Christian messages being passed to them (Benedict & Miller, 1994). Thus, the music used in contemporary worship is more appealing to the contemporary culture. In addition, since the majority of worship services are displayed on screens everyone has an opportunity to see and hear the message of the day.

Contemporary worship is also strong compared to the traditional way of worship in that it is engaging. In contemporary worship members are given an opportunity to ask or answer particular questions relating to Christianity. The question-and-answer sessions that have been adopted in contemporary worship assist in applying God's timeless truth to daily life. However, the questions and answers must be centered on biblical teachings (Gonzalez, 1996, P.56). Through such teachings the worshippers will understand the Bible and apply its message in daily worship services and general life situations.

In addition, the messages offered in contemporary worship are inspirational and encourage members of the church to develop a good relationship with God. In most cases, pastors use entertaining and thought provoking dramas that relate to the messages regularly presented to enhance the worship experience. It is through the use of inspirational messages that the contemporary worship attracts large congregations compared to the traditional ways of worship (Giuliani, & Roberts, 2004). Through reviewing literature one understands that spiritual leadership is necessary for the attainment of spiritual development. A pastor should lead by giving life meaning. Therefore, he or she should have a sense of calling.

CHAPTER FIVE: CONCLUSION AND RECOMMENDATIONS

Conclusions

In conclusion, leadership in any organization is very important because it involves directing others towards accomplishing particular assigned duties. It ensures the achievement of goals and objectives that have been initially set. In the church, leadership is essential because it enables churches and congregations to attain spiritual needs. Leadership in the church can be assumed by the pastor, church leader or any other person appointed or ordained to lead the congregation (Banks, 1980). Visionary leadership guides others in a spiritual way which in turn results in effective building of the church. For a church to grow efficiently the pastor must lead others towards attaining the spiritual needs of the church. Vision for church growth and leadership requires that a pastor or church leader clearly see the requirements of the congregation and articulate the issues affecting them. A church will grow when the congregation comes together to worship God and encourages each other towards attaining eternal life (Chant, 2012c, p. 67). Therefore, a church leader should create and sustain a vision for the church and the entire congregation. This chapter is very important because it introduces the requirements of visionary leadership for church growth and offers the significance of having a vision when planting, growing and expanding churches in the contemporary Christian world.

Planning and expansion of the church needs proper leadership that ensures spiritual direction for the congregation to achieve the churches mission, vision, goals and objectives. It is important for the pastor to build a vision that is inspiring and offers something new. As a leader it is crucial to map out the direction that will be taken by the church for it to grow and expand (Yancey, 2009). Therefore, a leader should have a vision that the church, even though started slowly, will grow and expand. By utilizing management and leadership skills the pastor will successfully guide the congregation in the right direction.

In most cases, churches face challenges when it comes to growth and expansion. Many pastors and church leaders have not utilized the right leadership skills and visionary strategies to see church growth, expansion, and to meet the spiritual needs of the congregation. A church's vision equals the destination that one aims to reach. As such the leader should develop steps that enable the church to reach the desired destination. It is important for the leader to emphasize the vision of the church and the action that will be taken to attain that vision. Furthermore, a balance ought to be created when the instructions or the directions of a church are being established.

The church leader should motivate all the members to seek spiritual solutions to the problems facing them (Baumgartner, 1990). Members of the congregation need to be encouraged to find spiritual and biblical solutions to the problems facing them. Through such a visionary strategy, a leader or a pastor should create an environment where members of the church can be highly motivated to worship and build the church as a team. An enabling environment creates positive actions towards making the vision more realistic for the church members to achieve (Giuliani, & Roberts, 2004). Furthermore, by creating an enabling environment, the church leader or a pastor is encouraging the church members to motivate others.

Knowledge ensures spiritual development, and spiritual development is crucial. For the ministry to carry out its functions well it is important for the leaders to have an understanding of how they can grow spiritually. The leader should understand the needs of his or her congregation. Visionary leadership is an important avenue for ensuring dissemination of spiritual messages (DeKoven, 2008). A pastor is required to develop spiritually before leading the congregation towards spiritual growth and development.

When a pastor has a vision he or she will provide the right message to the church and community members. For effective delivery of the message the pastor or a spiritual leader should encourage people to discuss how to grow spiritually.

Members of the church or the community should be encouraged to engage in Bible studies. It is an important duty of the pastor to ensure availability of materials that encourage spiritual development. A church or a community that aspires to grow and reach spiritual maturity focuses on missions (Von Campenhausen & Campenhausen, 2009). Growing churches involves establishing missions that spread the word of God. As the word traverses through different regions spiritual development is encouraged that provides an opportunity for Christians to attain spiritual growth and stability. Spreading the word of God should be done by the members of the church or the community.

A church can develop a sound philosophy for Christian education through engaging in spirituality development. The Christian education regarding faith development, spiritual development and growth involve people from different levels. When everyone encourages spiritual development and growth, the church will be much more effective and people will realize the existence of God.

In the current ministry, spiritual development is very crucial because it ensures a positive personal growth. Through spiritual development members of the church are encouraged to love one another. Therefore, as they love each other they also show love towards God who is the creator of everyone. Furthermore, a spiritually developed person recognizes the existence of God as the protector of their lives. Such is applicable in current church ministry because spiritual growth and development involves increasing the knowledge and understanding of God's word (Barna, 2000). It also involves doing everything possible to discourage sin. The church and community members will be provided with spiritual messages on how to live and lead righteous lives and decrease the engagement in sinful activities. Spirituality is the aspect of an individual progressively becoming stronger in his or her inner life. Spiritual development of the church ensures that one becomes happy and leads a vibrant Christian life (George & Bird, 1993). Arguably, it is the process of becoming more mature and having a good relationship with Jesus Christ and God. Spiritual development and growth is important for the prosperity of church members and community members (Scuderi, 2010). People should be encouraged to develop spiritual ways and uplift each other.

Spiritual development is important because it provides a foundation for members of the church and community members to trust and believe in God. People develop spiritually through the practice of solitude, simple living, submission, and prayer. A pastor ought to strive to develop spiritually so the church and community members will develop and grow spiritually as well.

Transforming the church and the community towards realizing spiritual development is very crucial (Gemignani, 2002). Research shows that transformation occurs in the individual's heart and mind. For spiritual transformation to be realized the pastors and the church leaders must listen attentively to the spiritual needs of church members. Such transformations will produce a positive society. Visionary leaders are the builders of a new dawn. Visionary leaders are important in every situation because they offer solutions to challenges that call for effective leadership. In Christianity and church growth leaders work with the power of intentionality and alignment with a higher purpose of ensuring members of the church become spiritually mature. Their eyes are set on the horizon of spiritual growth and fulfillment. Because they are prayerful, they view the big picture of the church, the challenges facing the church and how well they can handle those challenges through spiritual means.

Theology refers to the study of God's nature and the religious beliefs as they are systematically established. Theology assumes that God exists in some form including the physical form, the supernatural form, the mental form and the social realities form. Theologians try to explain the nature of God by following such characteristics and experiences. On the other hand, theological approach refers to teachings of Holy Scriptures and the interpretation of the components that best describes the nature of God. According to Mulholland et al. (2012), theologians try to explain the supernatural God by describing his characteristics including the physical form, and the social realities of how God relates with humanity. The Word is said to be without error, and the truth is God cannot lie. The Word's domain is founded on the death and the resurrection of Jesus Christ who rules all things. If one rejects this fundamental truth, then he or she rejects God Himself (Cranston & Williams, 1984). The core purpose of the Word is not to reveal the secrets of heaven but God's message which illustrates his creative authority and his redeeming love through his son Jesus Christ. God's wholesome relationship with his creation is established in his Word. Furthermore, the theology of the Word approach focuses pre-eminently on Jesus Christ the Person as the Living Word. Jesus Christ who is the Living Word is holy and upright. For church leaders to be effective, they need mentors. Mentorship is a very important virtue in the church. It is of great significance for the church leaders to look for mentors and works towards achieving church leadership principles based on values extracted from the mentor. A mentor is someone who sets worthy objectives, establishes effective strategies and implements the planned activities in a more effective manner. What a leader does matters a lot in church planting and growth. To be a good leader, one should follow the example of Jesus Christ. By following the example of Jesus Christ, a church leader will learn humility, that is, how to treat people with the heart of a servant. The leader will also learn the virtue of perseverance, that is, how to endure adverse circumstances or suffering without losing joy. A church leader, such as Pastor Paul Earl Sheppard, can be a very important mentor to a church who wants his or her church to grow. Sheppard has been preaching since his teenage period and has been in the pastoral ministry since the year 1982. He has been serving as associate pastor of West Oak Lane Church. His humility, principles and leadership skills has enabled the West Oak Lane Church grow and prosper. Therefore, when one chooses him to be his or her mentor, he will be in the position to grow and become a very good leader.

A church leader also needs to understand the bible. The heart of a leader requires a love that will get involved in the messes and struggles which are being faced by the church followers. By reading and understanding the bible, leaders will be in the position to pick

55

the most important topics which allow them to address those challenges. Understanding the bible is very important to a church leader in that he or she will get a clear understanding of the nature of the leaders. Furthermore, there will be a sense of self-awareness which is very important for any church leader. Therefore, a leader who understands the bible will follow the example of Christ as seen in the 1st Corinthians 11:1 where Apostle Paul says "Follow my example, as I follow the example of Christ." It is very important for the pastors and church leaders to understand what God requires them to do so as to ensure the needs of all the congregation have been adequately addressed.

Effective leaders also need to be likeable. All leaders fight to be at least liked and respected by the followers. However, leaders including the church leaders need to know that execution, getting the job and done at the right phase is very essential thus just trying to be popular. Church leaders ought to lead the congregation towards the right direction and adopting right leadership skills and knowledge. Visionary leaders who aspire to be liked by his or her followers should adopt leadership traits such as politeness, respectfulness and listening skills. Through such traits, an individual will boost the chances of leadership and success. It is of great significance for the leader to understand that effective and respected leaders do not have a big gap between what they say and what they do. Therefore, telling of the truth is very critical and mandatory than just telling people what they ought to hear as such results in a loss of trust in the leader among the congregation.

Secondly, the Word is the writings found in the Holy Scripture commonly referred to as the Bible. According to Bass & Briehl (2018), the Word proclaims Jesus Christ as the head of the church who reveals his father through the Holy Spirit of God. In addition, the Word responds to all needs of humankind and the entire creation. Moreover, the Word is both authoritative and redemptive. Defining leadership in any organization immediately raises questions regarding the mission, vision, and objectives of church planting. As a leader, it is crucial to understand what church planting needs to ensure well-coordinated efforts between church leadership and the congregation of the church. The leader such as the pastor or any spiritual leader ought to use prayer and biblical messages while handling problems facing the church. Through prayer, God will provide solutions to pertinent issues facing church planting, growth, and expansion. Spiritual people orient everything including their lives to God through continuous prayer (Wagner, 2010, P.44). A spiritual leader builds his life and that of the church in the word of God and prayer. An effective leader who trusts in the Lord will easily figure out challenges that might be faced by the church and then acknowledges the presence of the Lord when addressing such problems. Furthermore, God's word is very crucial in that it permeates all the doing and thinking of God. Therefore, he does not act within the human or worldly wisdom but through the use of spiritual scriptures to reveal the hidden challenges facing the church and possible solutions to such problems.

Recommendations

Research recommends that a spiritual leader or a church leader should be a visionary leader that aspires to grow and reach spiritual maturity focused in missions. Growing churches involves establishing missions that spread the word of God. As the word traverses through different regions, spiritual development is encouraged that provides an opportunity for the members to attain spiritual growth and stability. Churches that do not focus on mission establishment have stagnated. Therefore, it is essential for spiritual leaders to realize the importance of Christian missions and thus establish them in their churches or communities (Fletcher, 2006). Leaders should also develop a vision and missions which encourage members to become involved in nurturing the church.

Every leader who is visionary begins by following someone else's vision which gives him a blueprint of what is expected of him or her. The fundamentals of visionary practice develop the ability to lead and achieve the vision. Therefore, a future visionary leader submits to the authority that comes from God. A visionary leader is shaped by the strengths and limitations which are crucial to the vision and vision development. Visionary leaders are significant and important in growing a church. Visionary leaders have a compelling vision for their organizations. They can see beyond the challenges and the ambiguities of today and how they can inspire and empower the leaders of today and the leaders of tomorrow in the organization. It is important that visionary leaders ensure team members are provided with ample opportunity to work towards realizing the vision and mission of the church. Therefore, the church leader charts the course of the church and implements that course. Visionary leaders in the church do not control the members of the church. He guides them to work together to achieve spiritual nourishment and expand their services to those areas which have not been reached with the word of God. More importantly, visionary leaders provide freedom to members of the church to choose the best path to achieve the vision (Gast, 1961). The leader should also be transformational. People who utilized transformational leadership, in most cases, inspire staff through efficient and effective communication.

Furthermore, it is through the transformational leadership that church or spiritual leaders can effectively create desirable environments that include all the members of the church. The environment which is created by transformational leaders provides intellectual stimulation. A transformational leader can adopt various leadership principles during church planting, growth and expansion.

Principles of leadership are crucial in the management of different organizations. By adopting principles of leadership church leaders ensure growth and expansion of the church. There are different principles of leadership that can be adopted by pastors and spiritual leaders. Church leaders should understand that leadership is defined by behavior and not a position. To ensure the effective growth of the church pastors and other church leadership should adopt good behavior founded on the Christian faith. Church leaders are responsible for making decisions on how to plant, grow and expand the church. Through Christian behavior leaders understand the challenges facing their church and take the necessary steps in addressing those challenges. A church or a community that aspires to grow and reach spiritual maturity focus in missions.

Growing churches involves establishing missions that spread the word of God. As the word traverses through different regions, spiritual development is encouraged that produces spiritual growth and stability. Churches that do not focus on mission establishment have stagnated. Therefore, it is essential for the pastors and spiritual leaders to realize the importance of Christian missions and thus establish them in their churches or communities. Theoretically, the knowledge of leadership has been carrying out since time immemorial. Many scholars have carried out research regarding the dynamics of leadership and pastoral care. Visionary leadership theory is a theory that provides readers with the opportunity to learn how leaders abstract followers in order to inspire them to pursue shared goals. Furthermore, the theory also provides knowledge on how leaders can achieve beyond ordinary expectations through application of the right leadership skills and knowledge. It is an important theory that studies what inspires ordinary leaders to move to different levels of their expectations. The visionary leadership theory explains that leaders should have an inspiring vision and good behavior if they want to achieve more in the leadership roles. According to the theory, leaders should be in the position to understand the needs of the people he or she leads and try to provide effective leadership to make those being led comfortable and ready to follow such a leader. According to the theory, visionary leaders are found in every facet of the society ranging from the business institutions, religious organizations, community groups, sports teams and even the social change movements (Blair & Rivera, 1992). Furthermore, visionary leaders are found in different cultures, across gender lines and different organizational zones.

It is through the theory that vision is understood to be a leader's ideological statement of long-term, desired, long-term future for the institutions or organizations they lead. A vision explains the ideal future that the leader wants to establish. In most cases, it is articulated in what is a known as a vision statement. Visions enable the leaders to communicate the strategies of the institutions to the members of the institutions.

On the other hand, "A Dynamic Theory of Leadership Development" is a theory that explains that leadership refers to a developmental process that is based on the type of choice which is made by the leader. It further explains that good options are available and a visionary leader should choose the right choices to achieve the goals and objectives of the organization. However, the choices are made based on the world view looking for affiliations and looking for achievements. Additionally, leaders must understand that the choices they make should be organizational mission, vision, goals, and objectives. The theory seeks to answer questions such as "What?" "How" and "Why?" As a leader, it is significant to ask such questions to effective delivery of the services. The theory significantly presents important qualities that should be possessed by a leader. Those leaders who are aspiring will gain knowledge on how to remain progressive regarding developments. More importantly, leaders will have to understand their roles to ensure effective service delivery.

"The Theoretical Foundation of Pastoral Care in Christian Tradition" is an important theory that was founded with the aim of providing knowledge on the pastoral care and counseling. Counseling raises attention to the pastors to have an effective day-to-day delivery of the spiritual message to the congregation. According to the theory, pastoral care is an important aspect that connects the members of the church with their leaders. The theory explains that pastoral care stems from the Christian tradition (Blair & Rivera, 1992). Therefore, for the pastors to make correct translations in the message they deliver, they have to understand the requirements of being a pastor.

In connection, pastors should understand the theories to gain more knowledge on how to deliver a spiritual message to the congregation. Visionary leadership theory provides essential knowledge to the leaders on what they are supposed to do if they want to achieve important goals and objectives of the church (Nanus, 1992). A pastor should have a vision for the church and the congregation. Pastors who are visionless may not be in the position to effectively lead the churches and in most cases, they may fail to make the members of the church understand the existence of God. However, when leaders have a vision, they have the opportunity to understand the requirements of the church and thus provide effective leadership. Visionary leadership theory is an important theory that enables pastors to understand the significance of developing quality leadership skills to effectively carry out the designed roles in a more efficient manner. Furthermore, the theory explains that pastors should develop good behavior that enables him or her have a mutual relationship with the members of the church (Clebsch & Jaekle, 1994).

It is important for church leaders to direct the community of believers towards understanding the existence of Christ by engaging in deeper spirituality. Furthermore, a deeper understanding of the relationship between spirituality and church growth is the responsibility of church leaders. Bureaucracy makes the organization complex when management executes the activities in organizations. Rigid business rules and regulations inhibit the team from achieving its objectives and goals. Structure and strategy adopted by a business also make it complicated. It is reported that many organizations have a complex structure that requires too many employees to execute the activities. The complexity of an organization is also witnessed when the company develops complex business strategies. Accordingly, it is of great importance for the organization to have leaders able to run and accomplished business plans. Additionally, the methods used, and the products manufactured by a team also makes it complex. What is more, the planning, organizing and controlling processes makes an organization complex. As a pastor, it is important to encourage members to ask questions regarding spiritual issues and help them understand what it means to worship and why church participation is crucial to grow spiritually. Moreover, it is significant to involve the members in creative thinking and dramatize concepts relating to spiritual growth and development. Also, pastors should provide worship to enable people to understand the significance of participation in the church (Groeschel, 1984). During worship people develop spiritual ways and begun to form friends that results in the formation of spiritual groups that encourage others to join the church and grow together.

It is recommended that a church leader be spiritually mature and map out the direction for the growth and expansion of the church. As a leader, it is of great significance to utilize the management and leadership skills to successfully guide the team towards the right direction and effectively accomplish particular goals. Leadership is different according to the individuals who are assigned to lead others and based on the activity or the task that is to be accomplished. Leadership may relate to such aspects as political leadership, religious leadership and campaigning group leadership (Chant, 2012b, p. 77).

As a leader, it is of great significance to show visionary capabilities in order to bring change to the society and to those who are being led (Anderson & Anderson, 1975, P. 79).

Through visionary church leadership, the way of doing things in the church will be improved and thus the performance of the company or any other group would be significantly improved. Church leadership involves motivating team members to undertaking their assigned duties as required and follow biblical teachings that change them spiritually (Gookin, 1971). Thus, as a leader, one should set goals and objectives and inspire the team towards attaining them. Such a leader can utilize their emotional influence to motivate team members. However, after setting goals and objectives and directing team members towards them, the leader should monitor the performance of the team members and address the problems that might hinder the attainment of goals and objectives (Messner, 2003, P.24). In addition, good leaders ensure that the productivity of the team is uplifted. It means that church leaders should lay down groundworks for church members to follow and successfully build a living church.

Vision involves viewing the church or an organization through a diverse lens. As a leader of the church it is essential to clearly view where the church is going and ensure that all the set goals and objectives have been achieved holistically. A spiritual leader or a pastor must have passion, strength of will and knowledge to attain long-term goals and objectives. As a church leader, one should be in the position to inspire a team to attain spiritual goals and objectives. Therefore, the leader ought to be disciplined, creative and be an example others can follow (Chant, 2012d). The indigenous policy of planting churches began in the mid-nineteenth century when missionaries and other believers agreed that young churches should be self-propagating, self-governing and self-supporting for them to grow and expand. Therefore, the skill of planting and developing churches was extracted from these early principles. Many individuals were converted to Christianity and that resulted in the growth of churches that were planted by missionaries.

Evangelical methods were also important in developing the church and ensuring that the number of believers increased resulting in a community of believers. The culture of the communities where churches are planted should be adopted to enable the church to grow. Many churches after being planted have failed to grow because of poor mainstreaming of the local community's cultural values. Evangelical movements ought to take into consideration the cultural values of the society to ensure future growth of churches (Church Growth International, 2009). More importantly, the future growth of a church depends on how the Bible translates to new believers. Leaders of new churches have to teach members about the significance of building a good relationship with Jesus

Christ. They have to teach people what Jesus requires of them (Bettey, 1979). That will enable the building of a church that will faithfully follow commandments and ensure the increase of church members. A new church ought to engage in preaching and biblical worship to understand the gospel.

Most churches in contemporary society need to experienced revival. Revival is crucial because it ensures a spiritual awakening from the state of stagnation. Through revival a love for God and an appreciation of holiness will be renewed. (Block, 2009). Additionally, it ensures that believers are passionate about the word of God and church. When believers have a passion for God church growth is made possible. Revival is also essential in that it invigorates and sometimes deepens the faith of believers and opening of their eyes to the reality of Christianity in society (Meyers, 2003). Thus, the believers have a new beginning and eventually achieve church growth and expansion. Revival also generates the strength and will to live righteously and people live peacefully.

Churches need a renewal or commitment that ensures the resurrection of those who are not spiritually conscious. With revival people become acquainted with spiritual realities. They will examine themselves and their faith. It is through a revival that Christian believers acknowledge God and engage in prayer that produces church grow and expansion. In revival people return to God and work towards achieving what the church requires them to do. Personal revival provides an opportunity for the members of the church to accomplish the work God has ordained and they will win the hearts of the lost (McCoy, 2005). Through the revival missions, Christians embrace biblical authority that eventually makes them strong and eventually achieve what God desires them to achieve. Revival is an important opportunity where believers gladly ask God to renew their faith. Biblical teachings show that everyone is prone to making mistakes (Chorn-Pond & Ungar, 2012). Therefore, Christians might make mistakes that hinder other people from joining the church. In such cases, the growth and expansion of the church is negatively impacted. Revival is a way to teach believers the importance of resolving internal conflicts peacefully. Resolving conflicts peacefully ensures unity and eventually there will be few differences that might have shattered the church.

Leaders desire to see their churches grow, expand and meet the needs of the congregation. It is therefore significant for the church to understand how to achieve spiritual nourishment as a team. Scholars have argued that a church grows because God ordains it. But stagnant churches have become the norm in contemporary Christian society. The theologians must take into account the principles of planting and nurturing the church. Contemporary theology in most cases has sometimes focused on areas such as the gender equality in the community and the church. Some theologians argue that contemporary theology engages in encouraging feminists to indulge in religious leadership ignoring the stereotype that women cannot take part in leadership positions. Over the years much attention has been placed on men engaging in leadership positions leaving thus discriminating women in the society. According to various researches, such discriminations have extended to religious institutions. Furthermore, in contemporary theology, philosophical trends have also been a point of interest. More, issues relating to human rights, bioethics, faith in public and the environment have significantly been emphasized by the contemporary theologians (Olson, 2003). Every that is undertaken by the theologians is very significant because they focus on the attention of understanding the scripture and how God's word improves the relationship among the human being. Accordingly, the word of God is living and active. Furthermore, it does not change with time, and therefore, Christians through contemporary theologian are called upon to show love towards each other. They are expected to move around encouraging people to believe as the only creator of Heaven and Earth. The word of God spread by the theologians is very important because it enables people to grow spiritually and live worthy lives.

Contemporary theology and belief directly concern the individual believer and provides a basis for assurance of salvation. Fundamental issues relating to the deity of Christ, the work of redemption and also the experience of divine grace are undertaken through the contemporary theology. It provides that the standards absolute righteousness us very crucial for Christian relationship and engaging in other good things about Christianity. Bible is a very crucial tool that teaches about how God relates to the human beings and how he rules His creation. Therefore, by the spreading the word of Christianity, people will understand the existence of God. The authority over the creation demonstrates that God is the only Supreme Being and people should believe in Him. When an individual understands and believes in God, then such an individual gets an assurance of salvation.

The American way of life is a cultural aspect that must be considered my missionaries (Hesselgrave, 1980). They planted churches in various countries by implementing American culture. Therefore, the current churches in African countries were built on American culture because most of the missionaries were from America. Christians must realize that culture is a major factor when planting and nurturing the church.

The most complex problems which are encountered by theologians when planting new churches in different regions can be addressed through revival missions. Many churches have shut their doors because members and church leaders were not committed.

More revival missions are necessary to encourage the planting of new churches to improve the community. Even though America has many churches there remains a need to plant and grow more churches because of the growth in population (Ratliff & Cox, 1993). Additionally, the current and projected population growth rate in other regions of the world also indicate there is a great demand for planting more churches to cater to the needs of people. Through revival missions pastors and church leaders teach people the significance of planting new churches in different regions. The aspects of revival and church planting which the pastor can teach the congregation include training, discipleship and encouraging new members to become committed (Bloesch, 2008).

When church leaders or the pastor equips or trains the members to be committed, the church will grow to reach new areas. It is of great significance for the church to utilize biblical knowledge while leading the congregation.

It is also important for the church leader to develop spiritual stability that will enable the growth and expansion of the church. Pastors in many denominations face challenges. Such challenges may hinder the spiritual development of the pastor and make it difficult for the pastor to lead the congregation to spiritual development and maturity. As a pastor it is important to realize that there are challenges and issues which are faced on the spiritual journey. Therefore, challenges should not hinder a pastor from moving forward to attain spiritual stability. The journey of spiritual stability starts with spiritual formation and development (Langley & Kahnweiler, 2003). The essential aspect of spiritual development, maturity and eventual stability is to recognize the value of biblical sound teaching. Many pastors have not developed spiritually because of poor Bible study and prayer. They lack the knowledge that the Bible is an important instrument which should be utilized by the Christian to develop spiritually. When biblical knowledge is adopted by the church leader, then the church will grow successfully and eventually members of the church will attain spiritual nourishment.

REFERENCES

Abney, V. (2018). 21st Century Church Leadership and Pastor Preparation.

Anderson, P. A., & Anderson, P. M. (1975). The house church. Nashville, TN: Abingdon Press.

Banks, R. J. (1980). Paul's idea of community: The early house churches in their historical setting. England: The Paternoster Press.

Barna, G. (2000). Growing true disciples. Issachar Resources.

Barnard, T. C. (1993). Protestants and the Irish language, c. 1675–1725. The Journal of Ecclesiastical History, 44(2), 243-272. doi:10.1017/S0022046900015840

Baruth, M., Wilcox, S., & Saunders, R. P. (2013). The role of pastor support in a faith-based health promotion intervention. Family & Community Health, 36(3), 204-214. doi: 10.1097/FCH.0b013e31828e6733

Bass, D., & Briehl, S. (2018). On our way: Christian practices for living a whole life. Nashville, TN: Upper Room Books.

Baumgartner, E. W. (1990). Towards a model of pastoral leadership for church growth in German speaking Europe. Faculty Publications, 37. Retrieved from https://digitalcommons.andrews.edu/leadership-dept-pubs/37/

Beek, A., Borght, E. A., & Vermeulen, B. P. (2010). Freedom of religion. Studies in Reformed Theology, 19. Boston: Brill.

Benedict, D. T., & Miller, C. K. (1994). Contemporary worship for the 21st century: Worship Or Evangelism? Discipleship Resources.

Berkley, J. D. (2008). Leadership handbook of management and administration. Ada, MI: Baker Books.

Bettey, J. H. (1979). Church & community: The parish church in English life. New York: Barnes & Noble.

Blair, J. D., & Rivera, J. (1992). A stakeholder management perspective on strategic leadership. Strategic Leadership: a Multi-Organizational Level Perspective. Robert, L. Phillip and Lames G. Hunt, eds. Westport, CT: Quorum Book, 81-98.

Block, P. (2009). Community: The structure of belonging. San Francisco, CA: Berrett-Koehler.

Bloesch, D. G. (2008). Essentials of Evangelical Theology, 2 volumes. San Francisco: Harper and Row.

Brown, R. E. (1979). The community of the beloved disciple. Mahwah, NJ: Paulist Press.

Carter, J. C. (2009). Transformational leadership and pastoral leader effectiveness. Pastoral Psychology, 58(3), 261-271. Doi:10.1007/s11089-008-0182-6

Chant, K. (2012a). Better than revival. Harrisonburg, VA: Vision Publishing.

Chant, K. (2012b). Building the Church God wants. Harrisonburg, VA: Vision Publishing.

Chant, K. (2012c). Pentecostal pulpit. Harrisonburg, VA: Vision Publishing.

Chant, K. (2012d). Religion and philosophy. Cambridge University

Chant, K. (2013). Worship leader. Harrisonburg, VA: Vision Publishing.

Cheetham, R. (2000). Collective worship: A window into contemporary understandings of the nature of religious belief. British Journal of Religious Education, 22(2), 71-81. Doi:10.1080/0141620000220202

Chorn-Pond, A., & Ungar, M. (2012). An interview with Arn Chorn-Pond: Helping children in Cambodia through the revival of traditional music and art. In The Social Ecology of Resilience, 99-108. Springer, New York, NY. Doi:10.1007/978-1-4614-0586-3_10

Church Growth International. (2009). Church growth manual no. 15. Seoul, Korea. Retrieved from https://subsplash.com/paulawhiteministries/media/mi/+j4b8383

Činčala, P., McBride, D., & Drumm, R. (2017). Begger Better? How Church Size is Related to Church Health (&Growth).

Clebsch, W. A., & Jaekle, C. R. (1994). Pastoral care in historical perspective. Lanham, MD: Jason Aronson, Inc.

Conn, H. M. (1997). Planting and growing urban churches: From dream to reality. Grand Rapids, MI: Baker Books.

Costen, M. W. (2007). African American Christian worship. Nashville, TN: Abingdon Press.

Cowen, G. (2003). Who rules the church?: Examining congregational leadership and church government. Nashville, TN: Broadman & Holman.

Cranston, S. L., & Williams, C. (1984). Reincarnation: A new horizon in science, religion and society. New York, NY: Julian Press.

DeKoven, S. (1997). Supernatural architecture: Preparing the Church for the 21st century. Philadelphia, PA: Wagner Institute Publications.

DeKoven, S. (2008). Visionary Leadership. Harrisonburg, VA: Vision Publishing.

de Matviuk, M. A. C. (2002). Latin American Pentecostal growth: Culture, orality and the power of testimonies. Asian Journal of Pentecostal Studies, 5(2), 205-222.

Donald, W. A. (1970). Understanding church growth. Wm. B. Eerdmans Publishing.

Douglas, R. R. (2019). A Comparison of Resistance and Openness to Change in Church

Leadership and Church Growth through the 200 Barrier (Doctoral dissertation, Nyack College, Alliance Theological Seminary).

Elwell, W. A. (2001). Evangelical dictionary of theology. Ada, MI: Baker Academic.

Epes, T. F. (1948). Successful churches and better youth programs: Showing what to do and how to do it. Richmond, VA: T.F. Epes.

Erickson, M. J. (1998). Christian Theology. Ada, MI: Baker Academic.

Fee, C. (2018). Causes of burnout among church leaders: A qualitative phenomenological study of pastors.

Fletcher, M. (2006). Overcoming barriers to growth: Proven strategies for taking your church to the next level. New York, NY: Oxford University Press.

Fowler, J. W. (2008). Faith development and pastoral care. Minneapolis, MN: Fortress Press.

Francis, L. J. (2016). New directions in clergy psychological profiling. Theology, 119(2), 91-98. doi:10.1177/0040571x15615329

Freddoso, A. (1998). The openness of God: A reply to William Hasker. Retrieved from https://philpapers.org/rec/FRETOO

Garrison, V. D. (1999). Church planting movements. New York, NY: Oxford University Press. Retrieved from http://www.cpcoaches.com/pdf/cp/CPM%20BOOK.pdf

Gast, R. (1961). Churches in the general plan of the community. University of California.

Gemignani, M. C. (2002). Spiritual formation for pastors: Feeding the fire within. King of Prussia, PA: Judson Press

George, C. F., & Bird, W. (1993). How to break growth barriers: Capturing overlooked opportunities for church growth. Grand Rapids, MI: Baker Book House.

George, B. (2018). Relationship between the Emotional Intelligence of the Lead Clergy and Church Growth in North America (Doctoral dissertation, Virginia Tech).

Getz, G. A., Wall, J. L., Swindoll, C. R., & Zuck, R. B. (2000). Effective church growth strategies. Nashville, TN: Word Pub.

Giuliani, R. W., & Roberts, T. (2004). Leadership. New York: Hyperion Audiobooks.

Gonzalez, J. L. (1996). Alabadle! Hispanic Christian worship. Nashville, TN: Abingdon Press.

Gookin, D. (1971). Historical collections of the Indians in New England. Massachusetts Historical Society.

Gore, P. C. (2013). Ministry of the Christian Church. The Classics Us.

Groeschel, B. J. (1984). Spiritual passages: The psychology of spiritual Development for those who seek. Spring Valley, NY: Crossroad.

Hayward, J. (2018). Mathematical modeling of church growth. The Journal of Mathematical

Sociology, 23(4), 255-292. doi:10.1080/0022250x.1999.9990223

Hesselgrave, D. J. (1980). Planting churches cross-culturally: A guide for home and foreign missions. Grand Rapids, MI: Baker Book House.

Johnson, D. W. (1989). Vitality means church growth. Nashville, TN: Abingdon Press.

Johnston, R. K. (2009). Evangelicals at an impasse: Biblical authority in practice. Louisville, KY: John Knox Press.

Joo, B. (., Byun, S., Jang, S., & Lee, I. (2018). Servant leadership, commitment, and participatory behaviors in Korean Catholic church. Journal of Management, Spirituality & Religion, 15(4), 325-348. doi:10.1080/14766086.2018.1479654

Jordan, H. (2019). Leadership Factors That Influence Church Growth for Western North Carolina Churches of God.

Kirby, D. (2014). Fantasy and belief: Alternative religions, popular narratives and digital cultures. Abingdon, Oxon: Routledge.

Lai, S. L. (2016). To study the church growth of the Hong Kong Evangelical Church from 2003 to 2012.

Langford, A. (1999). Transitions in worship: Moving from traditional to contemporary. Nashville, TN: Abingdon Press.

Langley, W. M., & Kahnweiler, W. M. (2003). The role of pastoral leadership in the sociopolitical active African American church. Organization Development Journal, 21(2), 43.

Leithwood, K., & Jantzi, D. (2005). A review of transformational school leadership research 1996–2005. Leadership and Policy in Schools, 4(3), 177-199. Doi:10.1080/15700760500244769

Lienhard, J. T. (2011). Ministry. Wipf and Stock Publishers.

Lightner, R. P. (1995). Handbook of Evangelical theology: A historical, biblical, and contemporary survey and review. Grand Rapids, MI: Kregel Academic.

Lyall, D. (1994). Counseling in the pastoral and spiritual context. United Kingdom: McGraw-Hill Education.

Malphurs, A. (2004). Planting growing churches for the 21st century: A comprehensive guide for new churches and those desiring renewal. Ada, MI: Baker Books.

McCoy, L. S. (2005). Planting A garden: Growing the church beyond traditional models. Nashville, TN: Abingdon Press.

Messner, R. (2003). Church growth by design: A complete guide for planning and building churches to God's glory. New York, NY: Empire Group.

Meyers, I. P. (2003). This church is not appearing glorious, and it doesn't seem to be purpose driven: How to fix the broken church. New York, NY: Oxford University Press.

Mulholland, W. R., Anderson, D. W., & Anderson, D. W. (2012). Toward a theology of special education: Integrating faith and practice. Bloomington, IN: WestBow Press.

Mutia, P. M., K'Aol, G. O., & Katuse, P. (2016). Setting the Strategic Direction and it's Influence on Church Growth in Kenya. International Journal of Humanities and Social Sciences, 8(1).

Nanus, B. (1992). Visionary leadership: Creating a compelling sense of direction for your Ooganization. San Francisco, CA: Jossey-Bass Inc. Retrieved from https://eric.ed.gov/?id=ED350948

Olson, R. E. (2003). Tensions in Evangelical theology. Dialog, 42(1), 76-85.

Patzia, A. G. (2001). The emergence of the church: Context, growth, leadership & worship. Downers Grove, IL: InterVarsity Press.

Pinnock, C. H. (2001). Most moved mover: A theology of God's openness (Didsbury lectures 2000). Grand Rapids: Baker/Carlisle: Paternoster.

Ratliff, J. S., & Cox, M. J. (1993). Church planting in the African-American community. Baptist Sunday School Board.

Sanders, J. (1998). The God who risks: A theology of providence. Downers Grove, IL: InterVarsity Press.

Scuderi, N. F. (2010). Servant leadership and transformational leadership in church organizations (Unpublished dissertation) Retrieved from https://search.proquest.com/openview/a62c5e23fd675b82ff2e26a27014cdc4/1?pq-origsite=gscholar&cbl=18750&diss=y

Smith, C. (2002). Christian America?: What Evangelicals really want. University of California Press.

Smith, C., & Emerson, M. (1998). American Evangelicalism: Embattled and thriving. University of Chicago Press.

Strohbehn, U. (2016). Zionist churches in Malawi. Malawi, Africa: Mzuni Press.

Van Gelder, C. (2000). The essence of the Church: A community created by the spirit. Ada, MI: Baker Books.

Von Campenhausen, H., & Campenhausen, H. (2009). Ecclesiastical authority and spiritual power in the church of the first three centuries. Redwood City, CA: Stanford University Press.

Wagner, C. P. (2010). Church planting for a greater harvest: A comprehensive guide.

Eugene, OR: Wipf and Stock Publishers.

Ware, B. A. (2000). God's lesser glory: The diminished God of open theism. Wheaton, IL: Crossway.

Watt, L., & Voas, D. (2015). Psychological types and self-assessed leadership skills of clergy in the Church of England. Mental Health, Religion & Culture, 18(7), 544-555. doi:10.1080/13674676.2014.961250

Williams, M. (1994). Revisioning Evangelical theology: A fresh agenda for the 21st century. Pro Rege, 23(1), 35-36.

Williams, R. (2000). Christ on trial: How the Gospel unsettles our judgement. Zondervan.

Wofford, J. C. (1999). Transforming Christian leadership: 10 exemplary church leaders. Ada, MI: Baker Books.

Wong, P. T., Davey, D., & Church, F. B. (2007). Best practices in servant leadership. Servant Leadership Research Roundtable, School of Global Leadership and Entrepreneurship, Regent University, 7(1), 1-15.

Wright, T., & Wright, J. (1997). Contemporary worship. Nashville, TN: Abingdon Press.

Yancey, G. (2009). One body, one spirit: Principles of successful multiracial churches. Downers Grove, IL: InterVarsity Press.

APPENDIX A: LEADERSHIP INVENTORY

The ten point Likert scale values:

1: Almost Never   6: Sometimes
2: Very Rarely   7: Fairly Often
3: Almost Seldom   8: Usually
4: Once in a while   9: Frequently
5: Occasionally   10: Always

Questions:

1. I set a personal example of what I expect of others

2. I talk about future trends that will influence how our work gets done

3. I seek out challenging opportunities that test my own skills and abilities

4. I develop cooperative relationships among people I work with.

5. I praise people for a job well done.

6. I spend time and energy making certain that the people I work with adhere to the principles and standards we have agreed on.

7. I describe a compelling image of what our future could be like.

8. I challenge people to try out new and innovative ways to do their work.

9. I actively listen to diverse points of view.

10. I make it a point to let people know about my confidence in their abilities.

11. I follow through on promises and commitments I make.

12. I appeal to others to share an exciting dream of the future.

13. I search outside the normal boundaries of my organization for innovative ways to improve what we do.

14. I treat others with dignity and respect

15. I make sure that people are creatively rewarded for their contributions to the success of our projects.

16. I ask for feedback on how my actions affect other people's performance.

17. I show others how their long-term interests can be realized by enlisting a common vision

18. I ask "What can we learn?" when things don't go as expected.

19. I support the decisions people make on their own.

20. I publically recognize people who exemplify commitment to shared values.

21. I build consensus around a common set of values for running our organization.

22. I paint the "big picture" of what we aspire to accomplish.

23. I make certain that we set achievable goals, make concrete plans, and establish measurable milestones for the projects and programs that we work on.

24. I give people a great deal of freedom and choice in deciding how to do their work.

25. I find ways to celebrate accomplishments

26. I am clear about my philosophy of leadership

27. I speak with genuine conviction about the higher meaning and purpose of our work.

28. I experiment and take risks, even when there is a chance of failure.

29. I ensure that people grow in their jobs by learning new skills and developing themselves.

30. I give members of the team lots of appreciation and support for their contributions.
The following is a list of Question Numbers and the variable they
relate to 1, 6, 11, 16, 21, 26   Model the Way

2, 7, 12, 17, 22, 27	Inspire a Shared Vision
3, 8,, 13, 18, 23, 28	Challenge the process
4, 9,14, 19, 24, 29	Enable others to act
5, 10, 15, 20, 25, 30	Encourage the Heart

APPENDIX B: SEMI-STRUCTURED INTERVIEW QUESTIONS

1. What external factors, those outside of your church, do you believe have had an influence on the growth or lack of growth of your church?

2. What internal factors, those inside the church, do you believe have had an influence on the growth or lack of growth of your church?

3. What about you do you believe has had an influence on the growth or lack of growth of your church?

4. Would there be anything else you can think of that may have had an influence on the growth or lack of growth of your church?

ABOUT THE AUTHOR

Nulla malesuada neque diam, in aliquam libero tincidunt non. Nullam tristique, purus eu hendrerit sollicitudin, ipsum leo semper mauris, non feugiat purus nibh sed enim. Integer faucibus felis justo, vel dictum tellus tincidunt non. Vivamus in nulla sem. Vestibulum dignissim elit quis lorem malesuada mollis. Cras eget leo sed arcu feugiat aliquam. Sed vitae pharetra lacus. Aenean in viverra nunc, ac pharetra sapien. Suspendisse vitae nibh laoreet, elementum augue vitae, venenatis tortor. Vestibulum imperdiet nisl diam, eu dapibus ipsum ornare id. Praesent mauris dui, hendrerit ac lorem ornare, vestibulum pharetra magna.

Donec sit amet nibh fringilla, vulputate dui iaculis, tempus massa. Aliquam erat volutpat. Nullam dictum sit amet lectus id eleifend. Aenean a leo diam. In condimentum, orci sit amet aliquam iaculis, turpis ante tincidunt purus, sollicitudin tincidunt urna ante non mauris. Nam aliquam nulla sed ante scelerisque, in ultricies dui auctor. Pellentesque quis vehicula odio, id dapibus lectus.

www.website.com

www.ingramcontent.com/pod-product-compliance
Lightning Source LLC
Chambersburg PA
CBHW081643040426

42449CB00015B/3435